D0065969

COMPUTER MONOGRAPHS

General Editor: Stanley Gill, M.A., Ph.D.

Associate Editor: J. J. Florentin, Ph.D., *Birkbeck College, London*

2

A COMPARATIVE STUDY OF PROGRAMMING LANGUAGES

A
COMPARATIVE STUDY
OF PROGRAMMING
LANGUAGES

BRYAN HIGMAN

Professor of Computer Studies, University of Lancaster

MACDONALD:LONDON
AND
AMERICAN ELSEVIER INC.: NEW YORK

WILLIAM MADISON RANDALL LIBRARY UNC AT WILMINGTON

© Bryan Higman, 1967

First published 1967
Second impression 1968
Third impression 1969
First published in paperback 1969
Fourth impression 1970
Fifth impression 1973

Sole distributors for the United States and Dependencies

American Elsevier Publishing Company, Inc.
52 Vanderbilt Avenue
New York N.Y. 10017

Sole distributors for the British Isles and Commonwealth

Macdonald & Co. (Publishers) Ltd
49–50 Poland Street
London W.1

All remaining areas

Elsevier Publishing Company
P.O. Box 211
Jan van Galenstraat 335
Amsterdam
The Netherlands

Library of Congress Catalog Card Number 67-29193

Macdonald ISBN 0 356 02219 6
American Elsevier ISBN 0 444 19567 X

All Rights Reserved. No part of this publication may be reproduced, stored in a retrieval system, or transmitted, in any form or by any means, electronic, mechanical, photocopying, recording or otherwise, without prior permission of the publishers.

PRINTED IN GREAT BRITAIN

QA76
.5
.H49

CONTENTS

141087

I

INTRODUCTION

To non-specialists in the field, the phrase 'a programming language' is usually held to mean 'one of those things like Autocode, Fortran, Algol or Cobol, which are supposed to make programming easier'. Programming is drawing up schedules of instructions for a computer, to make it able to carry out a specified task correctly. Given a programming language, the instructions can be expressed in terms more like the English, or more like the mathematics (whichever you prefer), that we are accustomed to use, and there is a programme already written called the 'compiler' or 'translator', which will turn this painlessly into what you would otherwise have had first to write and then to punch for yourself with great difficulty. In some cases the translator does not even bother you with the translation, it just carries on and obeys it; this is called a 'load-and-go' translator. The combination of a language with a translator for a specific machine is called a 'system'. An alternative form of system — usually too slow to be practicable, but of value in special cases — reads what you have written straight into the machine, and there is an 'interpreter' also in the machine which is continuously looking at what you wrote and carrying out the processes implied by it.

All this is true but is too narrowly blinkered. The machines' own codes are just as much programming languages, and the writer of a compiler is accustomed to say that it translates from a 'source language' into a 'target language'. Buried inside some compilers there are 'intermediate languages'. Most translators today do more than translate; they also arrange to report back, not only on anything ungrammatical or meaningless in the original text, but also on difficulties which arise during execution, such as a division which looks (and usually is) all right, but which on some particular occasion turns out to ask for division by zero. This part of the system is known as the 'monitor'. A language has also the right to be judged *per se*, as a means for the communication of programming procedures between human beings, divorced from any translation or running systems; at this last level, natural languages should not be excluded.

The writer of a work on comparative linguistics has always to compete with the fact that few of his readers will be familiar with *all* the languages he refers to, and yet many of them are likely to be more

1

familiar with some one or more of them than he is himself — but not always the same ones. Since natural languages have their place in our study, and English has a sort of neutrality in this respect, we have not hesitated to use it as a source of illustrations when possible. Where something more mathematical is essential, it will be useful to have an equally neutral source.

1.1 A language for illustrations

For this purpose we may use a language which consists of the conventions of algebra, supplemented by the following symbols to provide the programming element:

$$: \quad ; \quad := \quad \textbf{go to} \quad \textbf{if} \quad \textbf{then} \quad \textbf{else}$$

The symbol $:=$ is the imperative equals, and occurs once in each assignment statement. That is, $x := -b + \sqrt{(b^2 - 4ac)}$ is an assignment statement which is to be obeyed, and when it has been obeyed then whatever value x originally had, it has now been given the same value as the expression on the right has. To obey $x_k := y_{k-1}$ we first see what value k has and then, for that value of k only, give x_k the value which y_{k-1} now has. The statement $x := x+1$ means that x is to be given a value one greater than its present value. Assignment statements are to be obeyed in the order in which they are written. A statement **go to** P means that the next statement to be obeyed is the one that has $P:$ in front of it. The symbol ';' separates statements from one another, and **if** . . . **then** . . . **else** may be taken at their face value. For example, we can calculate the value of e correct to p significant figures by

$$
\begin{aligned}
& x := 1; \quad y := 1; \quad k := 1; \\
Q: \quad & x := kx+1; \quad y := ky; \quad k := k+1; \\
& \textbf{if } y < 10^p \textbf{ then go to } Q; \\
& e := x/y
\end{aligned}
$$

This language is a subset of Algol with concessions to algebraic notation.

From time to time we shall use the phrase 'a higher-level feature' about some aspect of a language. By this we mean that it can be defined in terms of simpler concepts already in the language, and is introduced as a convenience rather than as a necessity. For example, we can define

if B **then begin** X; Y; Z **end**; W;

where B is a condition and X, Y, Z, W are assignment or go-to statements, as meaning

$$
\begin{aligned}
& \textbf{if } B' \textbf{ then go to } C; \\
& X; Y; Z; \\
C: & W
\end{aligned}
$$

where B' is the inverse condition to B (assumed available — i.e. if

2

'$=$' is in the language then so is '$\neq$'). **begin** and **end** are *statement brackets*.

1.2 Preliminary definitions

The foregoing paragraphs may be held to contain the definitions of such terms as 'system', 'monitor', 'load and go', as we shall use them. Certain other definitions will have to be discussed at length. But it will be advantageous to define here our use of certain terms which belong to the underlying subject of data representation; the following definitions are equivalent for most practical purposes to those in the standard glossaries, but the form in which we give them has certain advantages from the formal point of view as regards their logical relations.

A *digit* is
1. A mental concept with the property that it can assume any one of a finite number of states, or
2. Any representation of such a concept in physical form.

A *character* is
1. One of the states of a digit. When 'digit' is given the first of the above meanings, then the word 'character' in this sense may be qualified by the word 'abstract'.
2. Any representation of a digit in a particular state.

An *alphabet* is a complete set of associated representations of the states of a digit, i.e. a set of characters all in the same medium (or abstract) and with a one to one correspondence with all the states which the digit can assume.

A *numeral* is a character which has the semantic associations commonly given to the characters $0, 1, 2 \ldots 9$

A *character string* (often simply *string*) is an ordered sequence of characters — i.e. a sequence of digits, each in a determinable state — with a first and a last member and in which each member except the last has a unique successor and each member except the first has a unique predecessor.

A *message* is a character string in a semantically defined context — i.e. in a context which provides rules for determining a meaning for the string. If the rules are unsuccessful, we may refer to an illegitimate or abortive message.

A *code* is
1. A correspondence between two ways of using the alphabets of two digits or two ways of using one or more alphabets of the same digit such that corresponding messages convey identical information.

3

2. The rules stating such a correspondence.
3. *Machine code* is that use of strings in a certain alphabet which is interpreted directly by the control mechanism of a computer. This expression should be 'machine language', but is in too general use to be abandoned altogether.

Note that the effect of these definitions is to make '365' a three-digit number, each of its digits being decimal (having a ten-character alphabet). On a cricket scoreboard, digits are rectangular windows or cup-hooks; characters are distinctive marks on cloth or on pieces of tin (possibly including the blank as a character). Omitted from the above are those definitions which refer to the interpretation of strings of numerals in a place-significant manner; these are too universally understood to give rise to possible difficulties, though their application gives rise to problems.

One other term and its associated notation warrants inclusion here, though hardly required until Section 7. In order to talk *about* a language it is usually necessary to go outside the language, and particularly so when the language in question is a specialized one designed for a limited purpose. If the talking about is to be done with mathematical precision, it may be necessary to invent another language for the purpose, with symbols over and above those of the subject language. Such a language is called a *metalanguage*, its characters metacharacters, and so on. Just as our illustrative language in Section 1.1 used English words in heavy type to create some of its new symbols, so, as far as possible, we shall use English words in special brackets, < and >, for variables in the metalanguage; other types of metasymbol will be introduced as and when required.

1.3 Objectives

Even in April 1963 it was possible for *Automatic Programming Information* (Goodman (1963)) to produce a list of over thirty languages which had been implemented in Britain, and, since the ideal programming language has not yet been found, new ones are still appearing. But as a result of the experience thus gained we have reached the stage when it is possible to discuss a language in general terms, assessing it from the point of view both of the user and of the compiler-writer. A comparative study of programming languages must therefore be much more than a compilation of statements like 'Algol allows you to mix integer and floating point numbers but Fortran does not'. It must attempt to lay bare the underlying principles which distinguish a 'good' language from a 'bad' one. This can only be done tentatively at present. Consider that one speaker (Sproull, 1964) has told an American Congressional Committee that 'our goal is to permit the computer to accept English as we speak it', whereas most workers in the field insist that a programming language should be unambiguous. A writer once praised the summation convention in tensor calculus on the grounds that 'it makes you do useful things you wouldn't have thought of doing for yourself'. How many programmers would deem that a virtue in a language?

Perhaps the best that can be said is that a good language will

1. Use a standard character set;
2. Allow you, somehow or other, to do anything you want to do which can be defined in the context of your problem without reference to machine matters which lie outside this context;
3. Make it easiest to express the solution to your problem in terms which conform to the best practice in your subject;
4. Allow such solutions to be expressed as compactly as possible without risking the obscurity which often accompanies compactness;
5. Be free of any constructions which can give rise to unintentional ambiguities;
6. Permit the sort of ambiguity which is resolved dynamically, if the nature of the problem calls for this;
7. Take over without change as much as possible of any well-formed descriptive language which is already established in the field in which the problem originated;
8. Permit transcription — e.g. reading aloud, hand or typewriting as well as punched cards or tape;
9. Allow of easy apprehension, i.e. it should be possible to read other people's programmes *more* as one would a novel and *less* as one does an examination set book, than most *current* programming languages permit one to do;

and so on. These concern mostly the user. The compiler-writer is in the position of mediator between the machine designer and the user (except that he is terribly at the mercy of a *fait accompli* by the former). The features which make a language seem good to him are quite different. For example, it is advantageous to him if a message in the language can be interpreted without retracing one's steps. ('Two pages of the book . . .' seems clear enough, but has to be reconsidered if it continues '. . . of Psalms'. This sort of thing on the grand scale is very bad for the morale of a compiler.) But it is the opinion of the author that the next phase of development in computers will call for far greater concessions by machine designers to compiler-writers than the other way round, so that it is difficult to assess which of the compiler-writer's present difficulties will remain with us, and should be minimized by language designers, and which will shortly disappear.

1.4 Maintenance

It is an advantage of an artificial language that its inventor can say exactly what its rules are. If, after experience with it, it appears that it can be improved, or conversely that some of its users are abusing it, then it is necessary that somebody should be responsible for deciding what changes are justified, or how ambiguities should be interpreted, and for publishing its decisions. Frequently the inventor is unsuited, for one reason or another, to undertake this task, and if the language is an important one it may be passed to some committee at a national or international level. The committee is then said to be responsible for the maintenance of the language.

2

THE NATURE OF LANGUAGE IN GENERAL

A precise definition of language is an elusive thing, but we come fairly close to one if we say that a language consists of a set of objects called its vocabulary, which can be combined into linear strings in accordance with certain rules known as its grammar, for communication to a recipient with the intention of inducing activity in the recipient relative to certain specific features abstracted from a general situation. Any such string is, according to our previous definition of the term, a *message*. The activity to be induced in the recipient may be internal to it, a mere 'awareness' of the features communicated, in which case the message is said to be in the *indicative* mood, or it may involve external activity, in which case the message is said to be in the *imperative* mood, but this is a crude and inadequate distinction. 'Think on these things' is indicative by this definition, though technically imperative. A lot depends on where the dividing line between internal and external is drawn. Subject to one rider, however, it will serve for the moment, the rider being that it must be possible to communicate *potential imperatives*, with more of a 'briefing' than a 'command' character about them, the recipient being immediately 'aware' of them but acting on them only in response to an overt imperative at some later time.

This distinction is one that is only partially respected by natural languages. It is respected in the command

On the word 'fire' raise rifles, pull triggers, reload and order arms
. . . fire!

It is ignored at one's peril in telling a small child to 'Go into the kitchen and fetch . . .', since the child may well be out of earshot before it knows what it is to do when it gets there. An adult would realize the semantic incompleteness of 'Go into the kitchen', and, even though willing to do so, would probably say, 'What for?' before obeying. But one has seen a computer behave like a small child in this respect when presented with an incorrectly punched tape, and it is said that even adults have been known hypnotically to 'obey' the inscription on a curious object which read 'The Little Wonder Fuse Blower: Insert in mains socket and PRESS!'.

7

B

2.1 Natural and artificial languages

The associations which tie the vocabulary of a language to the features of the situations with which it deals, and thus determine the meaning of a string, are known as its *semantics*, and are usually completely conventional, even though the history of the language may show them to have a natural origin, and to this extent all language is highly artificial. However, it is usual to refer to some languages as natural and to others as artificial, meaning by the former those which possess the power of growth, and whose present form is the result of much evolution, and by the latter, ones which were created at a stroke and do not have this power of evolution. This is one sense in which Esperanto is an artificial language. Alternatively, we may define a natural language as one which is, or was, used somewhere, sufficiently for children to acquire its use in the natural course of development, without a conscious learning process. This raises interesting questions. Most children in civilized countries learn the numbers 0 . . . 9 in this way, and there may be more children in the world who have picked up elementary arithmetic in this way than there are children who have picked up, say, the language of some small African tribe. The language of elementary arithmetic is, in fact, a borderline case under this definition.

The relation between the above two approaches to the distinction between natural and artificial languages is not coincidental. Every language which is used as a means of communication between human beings will inevitably be required, sooner or later, to deal with situations of a hitherto unforeseen nature. As long as the two human beings understand each other they will not be put off by pedants complaining that they have dealt with the new situation by means of illegitimate extensions of the language. Each intercommunicating group will force the language to meet its own needs, whether or not it has received formal instruction as to what is legitimate and what is not. In particular, each successive generation of children picking up and using a natural language in the second sense, will introduce evolutionary changes and make it a natural language in the first sense.

So a language is bound to change, but change is not always for the better. Any change which tends to cut us off from the established corpus of literature is bad, and extensions which arise unnecessarily, because the language already has the means to deal with the new situation, come under this head. So do careless blurrings of finer distinctions, which have the result that one half-baked idea is now expressed where two crisply expressed ones existed before. Against changes like this, the pedants should have our support.

2.1.1 Evolution in programming languages

Programming languages are not exempt from this process, much

8

though this may be deplored in some quarters. But where programming languages are concerned, there is the complication that some of the communicating individuals are human and some are mechanical, and the latter are unable to apply the sensibility which the former possess in order to keep themselves abreast of evolutionary changes. Thus, on the one hand, use of these languages between human beings tends to enlarge and develop them, while on the other, the difficulty of 'teaching' a machine to 'understand' every idiom in a language has led to subsets and dialects of languages. In consequence, Fortran exists in Marks I to IV and in varieties such as Hartran and Madtran (versions in use at Harwell and M.I.T. respectively), and alongside Algol one has heard on the one hand of Smalgol and Balgol ('Small Algol' and 'Burroughs Algol' — both subsets) and on the other hand of Jovial ('Jules' own version of Algol' — so expanded as to be a mutation into a new family). An interesting development here is Xpop, for which see Section 15.2.4.

A further complication introduced by the machine derives from the variety of card readers, tape readers, teleprinters and the like which are their organs of communication, and the author has met at least one machine which 'could not read its own handwriting' — that is to say, its output was in a code different from any of those which its input was designed to accept. This complication we shall regard it as our duty to avoid as much as possible, except in Section 6 where we consider it in some detail.

2.2 Syntax and Semantics

The complete description of a language involves its grammar and its semantics, the former often being divided into accidence and syntax. There is no hard and fast dividing line between these three. Accidence recognizes a possible internal structure to the vocabulary, as when 'come' has variants 'comes' and 'came'. So far, those programming languages which have not tried to base themselves on English have been very successful in avoiding anything of this sort. One might, perhaps, think that in a programming language numbers were the equivalent of words, and their internal structure certainly matters, but Algol, for example, builds numbers up from numerals, etc, in its formal syntax, and only in the recent input/output proposals for this language (in the identifiers 'output1', output2', etc) does anything even resembling accidence find a place.

Again, considering syntax and semantics, one might think that meaning played no part in determining the grammatical structure of a sentence, yet meaning determines our immediate analysis of

Time	flies	like	an	arrow
noun	verb	adverbial	article	noun
subject		preposition		

9

as is shown (Pfeiffer, 1960) from the fact that we equally immediately apply a different analysis to

Fruit	flies	like	a	banana
noun	noun	verb	article	noun
used adjectivally				

A somewhat different situation which we shall discuss again in Section 7.1.1 occurs in the different interpretations in

1. Your son hates games; John's hates work.
2. Your hates are ineffective; John's hates work.

2.3 The communication of algorithms

A programming language is distinguished from other languages in that its purpose is to communicate 'algorithms', that is, organized sequences of instructions. The oldest algorithmic language in the world is probably that used by Euclid for the description of constructions, as in the first proposition in his first book, which runs thus in English:

To describe an equilateral triangle on the given straight line AB.
From the centre A at the distance AB describe the circle BCD.
From the centre B at the distance BA describe the circle ACE.
From the point C at which the circles cut one another draw the straight lines CA and CB to the points A and B.
Then ABC shall be an equilateral triangle . . . (here follows a proof of the validity of the construction) . . . and it is described on the given straight line AB.

The subject matter of this language comes very close to that required for machine control, for which the modern programming language Apt has been constructed. The most widely used programming language, if we admit organized sequences of instructions for control purposes as well as for computation, is probably the one in which the following extract is written:

Using No. 11 needles cast on 130 sts.
Work in K.1, P.1, rib for $3\frac{1}{2}$ in.
Next row Rib 9, (inc, in next st., rib 6) 16 times, inc. in next st., rib to end (147 sts.)
Change to No. 9 needles.
1st row P.5, * (K.4, P.3,) twice, K.1, P.2, K.1, P.3, rep from * to last 16 sts., K.4, P.3, K.4, P.5.
2nd and every alt. row K.5, * (P.4, K.3) twice, P.1, K.2, P.1, K.3, rep from * to last 16 sts., P.4, K.3, P.4, K.5.
3rd row P.5, * (K.4, P.3) twice, C.3, P.3, rep from * to last 16 sts., K.4, P.3, K.4, P.5.
5th row as 1st row.
7th row P.5, * C.7, P.3, C.3, P.3, rep from * to last 16 sts., C.7, P.5.

9th row as 1st row.
11th row as 3rd row.
12th row as 2nd row.
These 12 rows form the patt.
Continue in patt. until work measures ...

Experienced programmers will detect in this extract such features as bracketed sub-expressions, labels, and iterative loops terminating both on counts and on 'computed results', and in one instance a 'built-in check'. It also shows a hint of the 'procedure' or 'subroutine' with parameters, since 'C.3' and 'C.7' are defined earlier as

> Work across next 4(11) sts., as follows. Slip next 3(7) sts., on to cable needle and leave in front of work, K. next st. (K.4), slip 2(3) sts. from cable needle on to lefthand needle and Purl, K. the st. (K.4) from cable needle.

2.4 Nature of computation

But although we ought, perhaps, to confine our study to languages which describe computational processes, emphatically we must not be too restricted in our ideas of what constitutes a computation. It is true that there is a tendency to think of computation in terms of numerical work. But viewed against the background of mathematics as a whole, computation takes on a rather different appearance; it becomes that part of mathematics which is concerned with 'getting answers', as opposed to analysing and deepening our understanding of abstract relations in general. Everything now turns on what sort of answers we hope to get. The process by which we obtain $x = (c - b)/a$ from $ax + b = c$ is as much 'getting an answer' as is the one by which we obtain $x = 4$ from $3x + 2 = 14$. Furthermore, it is difficult to deny this same status to a successful response to a challenge in the form *Given the axioms . . . find a proof that . . .*, particularly seeing that computers have been programmed to do this. Each new discipline, such as 'Boolean algebra', 'Propositional Calculus', and so on, sets its own slant on what it means by computation. Finally, the processes involved in

$$x = (c - b)/a = (14 - 2)/3 = 12/3 = 4$$

namely, substitution and reduction, are so close in nature to those which would reduce

> Your reply should be addressed to *(the local offices of the appropriate ministry) (your local consular official).
>
> *Strike out whichever does not apply

to the form

> Your reply should be addressed to '6, Sunset Gardens, Shortwick'.

that again, the same machine can be programmed to do either, and it is manifestly wrong not to see that 'computation' covers both.

11

For these reasons, we shall regard computation as any form of character manipulation according to prescribed rules, while giving pride of place to those particular rules which, for example, permit the character string '26+5' to be replaced by the shorter string '31'. This still leaves a few details outstanding. Note that as linguists we are not concerned with either the accuracy or the efficiency of any algorithms which may be expressed in any of our languages, but only with the accuracy or efficiency with which the language describes or expresses those algorithms. Thus we have no moral duty to prevent a programmer from getting his machine into a tight loop because, by a slip of the pen, he wrote *R:* **go to** *R;* when he meant *R:* **go to** *P;* although we are concerned with whether, when he has done so, the language makes it easy for him to find and correct such a slip. But sometimes the exterior situation may appear to be wider than our definition allows for, as, for example, when a computer controls an industrial process. Such cases are covered by the definition we have already given for 'character', which allows characters to be followed through a variety of transformations, but effectively defines the limits of the computational system in a control situation as at the digitizers or digital-to-analogue converters.

2.5 Pure procedures

In one curious way, this extended concept of computation brings us full circle historically. The earliest machines were designed to operate upon numbers, and their instructions were coded into numerical form; now we write our instructions in a larger and more convenient character set, but permit the whole of this character set as potential participants in our operands. It used to be claimed that *because* instructions were numerically coded, the machines could operate upon their own programmes, but we can now see that this is only a half truth. It was the numerical coding which led us to appreciate the possibility, but the possibility itself is of wider application.

However, although most programmes are modified by the system into a more convenient form while still in the potential imperative state, it seems that it is unnecessary to be able to modify a programme which has become overtly imperative, provided that our languages possess a certain flexibility (which the earliest ones did not), and modern practice is all in favour of the *pure procedure*, or sequence of instructions which does not modify itself. Many languages admit no other. The original reason against impure procedures was the pragmatic one that if errors have been made in writing them, these errors are far harder to track down if the procedure has been allowed to alter itself. More recently a second reason has appeared in the possibility that certain routines may be simultaneously in use by different users, who cannot be allowed to change them in ways detrimental to each other. It may therefore be worth while spending some time in considering the nature of the flexibility required. Although it appears in various guises in different contexts, essentially it would seem to be the power to select an operand which cannot be named explicitly at the time of writing the programme. For a formal investigation which covers this point see Elgot and Robinson (1964).

By the time a programme comes to be obeyed by a machine it is in 'machine language'. The early machines used a language whose grammar was simplified (to make the engineering simple) to the point of considerable inconvenience. In effect all such grammatical devices as pronouns and relatives were eliminated, also dependent clauses of any kind. The use made of the power to alter the programme most often took a form which we can paraphrase as follows (though the analogy must not be pressed too far). Faced with a question like

On what river does the capital of England stand?

this question would be broken into the two steps

What is the capital of England? . . . On what river does it stand?

and then, being up against the lack of any equivalent to 'it', into the following three steps

What is the capital of England . . . Write your answer in place of 'Erewhon' in the following sentence. . . . On what river does Erewhon stand?

so that by the time the machine came to answer the final question, it had been modified into 'On what river does London stand?'. An example in actual machine code occurs in Section 9.1.

A number of devices introduced into machines at various times would all seem to be alternative ways of overcoming this difficulty. It must be remembered that the directions taken by these developments were often dictated by engineering considerations not easily reflected in this paraphrase. The B-line technique amounted to the two-step system:

What is the capital of England (write your answer on your scratch-pad)? On what river does . . . stand (fill in the blank from the scratchpad)?

The *obey* technique involved writing the modified *order* on the scratchpad (not modifying it *in situ*) and replacing the final instruction by 'Answer the question on the scratchpad'. Finally there was the indirect address technique, which, by giving access to the contents of the contents of an address, allows the programmer to write 'the name of the name of' whatever it is he requires, and in this way comes much closer to the form of the original question. Of these three, the B-line technique has been the most popular, probably for two reasons. First, it takes little or no time to implement, compared with the extra store accesses required by the other techniques. This

13

could change with the state of the art in engineering. Secondly, it is wider in scope than our present description would imply, though it is less flexible in this respect than the 'obey' technique. In particular, as is well known, owing to the additive process which it employs, it can be used to select the kth member of a set (e.g. the component x_k of the vector x) by storing the set in consecutive locations and writing its initial address in the instruction and the suffix in the B-line (or *vice versa*). Here we return to the realm of linguistic study, for we may remark that the abilities of oblique reference (or indirect addressing) and of being able to write an algebraic suffix, are properties which belong to a language rather than to the machine it is implemented on, although if the machine code does not also possess them, then the implementation may be exceedingly inefficient.

2.6 Classification of Languages

The newcomer to the subject may well ask why there are so many languages. The primitive languages *had* to take into account how the machines worked. When broken down into steps at this level, 'Eat your breakfast' starts with 'Open your mouth' if talking to a child, but with 'Open your beak' if talking to a pet parrot. But for this very reason, these languages could express everything that the machine was capable of doing. Nevertheless, it is because man has the ability to absorb detail into more generalized expressions (thus avoiding being bogged down by it) that man has made progress, and so it was inevitable that more sophisticated languages should arise. When they did, a problem arose to which the following is an analogy. Suppose a typewriter were produced which had words instead of letters on its keys. Then it would be much faster and more accurate in use, but limited to the subjects covered by the chosen vocabulary, unless the ability to fall back on the letters was retained. So it was with programming; either the ability to do *everything* that the machine could do was sacrificed, *or* a loophole was left to fall back on machine language. And correct though the latter was in principle, in practice it meant that one still had to know whether one's machine had a 'mouth' or a 'beak', and while one was learning this (if one did not give up instead) it was almost easier (and often more congenial) to write a new language for the new subject.

Today the problem is a different one. Every language is to some extent multi-purpose — because, for example, in a language designed for numerical calculations it still pays to be able to manipulate letters in order to produce an output which carries a few words of explanation and is not just a maze of numbers, while in a purely literary language it is still as well to be able to compute that the fifth line is three after the second! Should we not then work towards a genuinely all-purpose language? There are objections to this, but they are mostly met if the language is so designed that users need not

14

learn more of it than they require for their particular type of problem, and if behind the language there is an underlying structure which guarantees that systems need not waste time eliminating alternatives which such a user will never avail himself of. But this is not the only efficiency problem; there is a more serious one which we can illustrate by an example. Most machines represent integers in binary form, or in binary coded decimal using a 1,2,4,8 weighting. On such machines much the quickest way of determining whether a number is odd is to form the logical 'and' function between unity and the number; this will be zero for even numbers and unity for odd ones. But this will not work if the machine uses a 1,2,2,5 weighting, or 'excess three' representation. The programmer is supposed to be protected from the need to know which representation the machine uses, and the language will probably forbid him to use logical functions on numerical data in consequence, so that he will be reduced to the exceedingly inefficient process of seeing whether double the integral part of half the number is equal to the original number! One answer to this is to make the function *odd*(n) a system defined routine, implemented in different machines in different ways. But it will be a long time before we have worked out which are the processes whose efficiency is so system dependent that they ought to be defined in this way.

Another reason for the multiplicity of languages is that different attitudes to the problems involved have produced different types of languages. Some have groped their way towards the same methods of expression as are already familiar in natural languages, including among the latter the language of mathematics. These have tried to make their semantics completely independent of the machine. Others have aimed more at a generality of expression within the limitations of a particular machine or group of machines. Others have given particular attention to making allowance for the fact that computation is not exactly a *typical* everyday activity, and that therefore the best grammar for a computational language is likely to differ from that of natural languages. Two subdivisions must be recognized here, *procedural* languages, which recognize explicitly the sequential nature of most computational processes, and *functional* languages, which acknowledge only the one imperative 'evaluate', which can be left implicit, thus

(evaluate) $ax^2 + bx + c$ where a = 2, b = -3, c = 1, x = 0,1,2...20.

In some cases these represent trends, and not all languages have gone to an extreme in these matters. One particular problem was acute enough to give rise to a separate group of languages. In purely numerical work, the length of an operand, whether decimal or binary, can be kept within reasonable limits, but in other problems this is not so; as one example, every sixth-form mathematician knows

15

the outrageously long expressions one can get by differentiating quite a harmless looking function. These problems gave rise to list-processing languages, but the most recent trend has been to incorporate list-processing techniques into other types of language. (Giving the 'value' of x as 0,1,2. . . 20 is an example of this.)

2.7 The role of names in a programming language

The 'external world' to which a message in a programming language is related by its semantics is a peculiar and restricted, not to say introspective, affair, since it consists of character strings like the message itself, though not necessarily possessing any great semantic content in the language. (One cannot say more than this owing to the great disparity in semantic possibilities between the languages themselves.) One feature which, since it is a feature of computation itself, is found almost universally, is a three-fold division into input (data), output (results), and working space (temporary intermediate results), but even this is obscured in function languages. It will be advantageous to use the abbreviation *E-object* for an object in the *external* world, and *L-object* for an object in the *language*. The essential feature of the computational situation may then be described by saying that each E-object referenced by the message has

(i) a name (at least at all appropriate times) which is an L-object and which is used in the message, and

(ii) a value (which may be initially indeterminate)

Values are also L-objects, but the value of an E-object is not an object in the message which constitutes the programme (even though an identical object may occur in the message); rather it is something 'assigned' to the E-object by an imperative in the message.

In some languages (Autocode, for example) there is a comparatively fixed set of names, but in others (Fortran, Algol) the message may create them at will, and in this case, in a real computer, it is preferable to regard the name as prior to the E-object, which is created by associating a storage location with the name. The exigencies of this situation have led to a confusing multiplicity of uses of the word 'defined', and we shall try to avoid this by introducing alternative terms for some of the uses. We shall say that

1. A string is defined if its semantics are determinable. If the string is a name, its semantics are to that extent already determined, though they can be more precisely determined if we also know what sort of object is referred to. Thus a string may be 'more' or 'less' defined.

2. A name is 'sited' if there exists a corresponding E-object, otherwise it is 'siteless'. The E-object may be called its site.

3. A site is 'filled' if a value has been assigned to its name, 'void' otherwise. A name is 'filled' or 'void' if its site is.

16

Thus the string $x := y$ is incompletely defined if y is void, and still less defined if y is siteless; it is clear what it intends us to do but far from clear what will happen if we try to do it. The usage which must be deprecated is that which describes a *value* as 'defined' or 'undefined'. (Note: when names refer to pushdown stores, the need for care in these matters is even greater.)

Names can also refer to objects which are a part of the message itself — either values which are introduced by being embedded in the message, or more genuine parts of the message as such. Impure procedures are only possible if the grammar of the language (a) makes provision for names of the latter type, and (b) makes provision for assigning new values to these names, and in general, procedural languages need the former provision (for **go to** instructions) but avoid providing the latter. A name which refers to a part of the message as such is, roughly, what is usually called a *label*, although attempts to define this term strictly will reveal variations in its use (e.g. does it indicate a 'part of' the message or a 'point in' the message?). However, the concept of a name in computing theory is more complex than even the foregoing review would suggest. In the following sections we consider a number of subjects of general importance, and return to the theory of names after certain further foundations have been laid.

3

RECURSION

Experience in trying to teach the fundamentals of programming and of programming languages suggests that the concept of recursion is one which presents peculiar difficulties. In particular, programmers with considerable elementary experience seem to find it difficult to distinguish recursion from iteration, and, when they succeed in this, they find it difficult to see what the value of recursion is. The latter is not altogether surprising in view of the fact that in numerical work it often happens that a process is most efficiently performed iteratively even when there are advantages in defining it recursively. In other fields, however, this is not necessarily the case.

Iteration is the repeated performance of something until some condition is met, each performance being carried to completion, the condition being examined, and a new performance commenced if the result is unsatisfactory. In contrast to this, recursion involves a self-nesting; the performance is not carried to completion before the condition is examined, instead, the condition is examined within the performance and, if the result is unsatisfactory, the whole performance is asked for again as a subroutine of the as yet uncompleted original one. This description applies to recursive procedures, but the concept is also applied to definitions and structures. If we look at all three we shall have a surer grasp of the situation.

3.1 The nature of recursion

To see the two processes at work procedurally, consider two ways of finding the sum $f(1)+f(2)+ \ldots +f(n)$. In the first we define a subroutine

add term: add $f(k)$ to S, reduce k by 1, and return

Now we write

Set S to zero and k to n.
I: Plant a return link to J and transfer control to 'add term'
J: If k is not zero go back to I.

We thereby perform 'add term' n times, successively and independently, only one link being in use at any time; this is iteration. In the second we define

18

Sum(f, k) as equal to 0 if k = 0,
  otherwise equal to f(k)+Sum(f, k – 1)
And now we can simply ask for *Sum(f, n)*. Consider the case when *n = 2*. We plant a return link to whatever we want to do after the evaluation and transfer control to this definition. This causes us to evaluate *f(2)* and then calls for the evaluation of *Sum(f,1)* to be added to it. So we must store away *f*(2), plant another link, and re-enter the definition. This leads to evaluating *f*(1), again storing it away and planting a third link before entering the definition a third time to evalutate *Sum(f,0)*. But this is zero, so we come out of the definition using the link planted for this use of it, add the zero to *f*(1), again exit using the second link, add our '0+*f*(1)' to *f*(2) and make a final exit. This is recursion; our uses of *Sum* were not successive and independent but nested, and our three links were all held simultaneously and referred to on a 'last planted, first used' basis.

A curious feature of this example is that it is much less convincing if the definition is revised by reversing the order of the addition and making it *Sum(f,k – 1) + f(k)*. The effect of this reversal is far from trivial in the amount of information which has to be stacked away.

As an illustration of recursive and iterative structures, we may consider two English sentences. 'I came, I saw, I conquered' is an iterative structure inasmuch as three similar units occur successively as parts of the whole. (Inasmuch as the units are themselves sentences, it is recursive.) The sentence 'I said you think he is mad' is a recursive structure. I speak in sentences, so a sentence 'I said . . . ' will have a complete sentence as the object of 'said'; likewise you think in sentences. The result is that in a sequence of only seven words we have a sentence within a sentence within a sentence! Some more horrible examples are given later.

Finally, in the field of definitions, our definition of *Sum(f,k)* is a recursive definition because it defines *Sum* to a certain extent in terms of itself. The concept of iteration is less straightforward here, but generally speaking the iterative equivalent of a recursive definition would seem to be a form which uses the unsatisfactory device of a string of dots in the middle. A recursive definition must always contain one non-recursive alternative, or it becomes circular in the vicious sense, just as an iterative process must contain some means of 'getting out of the loop' — whether by requiring a number of iterations which can be shown to be finite, or by requiring an exit when a convergence test has been satisfied which it can be shown will be ultimately satisfied. This necessary criterion of validity (and a corresponding one for recursive definitions) need not hold, however, for all conceivable values of the argument of a function; if it does not, then the function is undefined for values for which it does not hold. For example, one would not necessarily expect an iterative process for square root to converge for negative values of the argument.

19

3.2 Applications of recursion

Our summation example is fairly typical of the situation in numerical work, in which the *recursive definition* is often neater, but the *iterative process* both looks and is more satisfactory in use. In consequence we must think of recursion as having two main spheres of importance.

The first is somewhat theoretical, and is that recursive definitions are the basis of the whole modern theory of computable functions (see, for example, Davis (1958)). For the sake of a later illustration, we sketch the beginnings of this. It is assumed that the *successor function* — call it $S(x)$ — exists for every positive integer and zero; it is $x+1$, of course, except that at this stage '$+$' has not been defined. Then the *predecessor*, $P(x)$, which will equal $x - 1$ when '$-$' has been defined, is defined as

$P(x) = P'(x, 0)$ **where**
$P'(y,z) = $ [**if** $S(z) = y$ **then** z **else** $P'(y,S(z))$]

This starts z at 0 and 'successorizes' it until its successor is x and then seizes it as the answer. The sum of two numbers is now

$Sum(x,y) = $ [**if** $y = 0$ **then** x **else** $Sum(S(x),P(y))$]

and the difference

$Diff(x,y) = $ [**if** $y = 0$ **then** x **else** $Diff(P(x),P(y))$]

But these processes can run into trouble. $P(0)$ will hunt for ever through the positive integers seeking a predecessor to zero, and if $y > x$ then *Diff* will reach a stage at which it calls for $P(0)$. For this reason *Diff* is said to be only partially computable (over the positive integers). There are various ways (which do not concern us) out of this impasse, and it has been shown that it is possible to define in this way every function which a computer can compute (including the rational approximations to transcendental functions, etc), and to provide a basis for demonstrating that there are some things it cannot do. Although most of these lie outside our scope, some of its results concern us. For example, there is the question of the 'decidability' of a language, which we explain in Section 7.3.

The second important use of recursion arises because the situation in numerical work is not altogether typical. In particular, procedures for analysing structures which may be recursive are most efficient if they themselves are recursive, and they must at least incorporate features which would be unnecessary in the absence of recursion in the data. In brief, we saw that an unlimited, last in first out, store for links and intermediate data is required by a recursive procedure, and most translators which are not written as recursive procedures seem to find it expedient to use a similar list or lists for temporary storage of some part of the primary data (i.e. of the message being translated) instead. Thus although recursion may be a luxury, even an extravagant luxury, in languages whose primary field is numerical, this is far from the case in general, and in languages for writing compilers and translators in particular.

3.3 Miscellaneous comments

It may also be worth mention that there are certain functions which are easily defined recursively but which cannot be defined in terms of ordinary algebraic expressions. Newell (1961) cites as an example, referring to Perlis (1959) and Kleene (1952), Ackerman's function, defined over the positive integers and zero by

$$A(m,n) = \text{if } m = 0 \text{ then } n+1 \text{ else if } n = 0 \text{ then } A(m-1,1)$$
$$\text{else } A(m-1,A(m,n-1))$$

The nearest one gets to an algebraic definition of this function contains exponents connected by a string of dots!

Once a computer is programmed to handle recursive structures as such, and not, for example, as first, second, third level occurrences with no provision for a fourth, it is not worried in any way by the number of levels involved. (Store size sets a limit, of course, but this is never likely to be reached in sentence analysis problems, where limits are set by the length, and not the value of the input data.) However, although natural languages have a recursive structure, our ability to handle this feature seems to be restricted, especially when the outer structures surround the inner ones. (In 'I said you thought he was mad' they all end together, and all the return links can be taken in a single jump. See also Section 7.5.) Miller (1965) quotes two examples. In the first, sentences are nested, and only to one level more than in our simple example, but the links have to be recovered one by one. This is

> The audience who just heard, 'The person who cited, "The king who said, 'My country for a horse,' is dead," as an example is a psychologist,' are very patient.

In the second, relative clauses are nested. In the form

> She thanked the producer who discovered the novel that became the script that made the movie that was applauded by the critics,

each clause drops a level of subordination but is not embedded in the strict sense of being surrounded on *both* sides by its superior. Truly embedded it becomes practically unintelligible, even with the help of two forms of brackets:

> The movie (that the script [that the novel (that the producer [whom she thanked] discovered) became] made) was applauded by the critics.

Our tolerance limit seems to be at about the second level:

21

The novel, that the producer (whom she thanked) discovered, became the script . . .

But a little further fooling in this direction suggests that it is rather easier to keep control if, by using distinct constructions (even ' . . . that . . . which . . . whom . . . ' is slightly easier than ' . . . that . . . that . . . that . . . ') we can make the burden on the memory less purely quantitative. The moral would seem to be that easy apprehension of the meaning of a text in a programming language will be assisted by the deliberate provision of what Strachey (1963) would call 'alternative varieties of syntactic sugar'.

4

POLISH NOTATION

A number of languages are based on a concept known as Polish notation; this has advantages for machine codes but is difficult for human digestion. It is so called because it was first introduced by the Polish philosopher Lukasiewicz in connection with the formulae of symbolic logic. A variation more properly called 'reverse Polish' is more popular today in computing circles.

When an operator occurs *between* its operands, as in $a+b$, it is described as *infixed*. Evaluation of an expression such as

$$3 \times 5 + 7 \times 11 \qquad \text{(A1)}$$

must pay due attention to the superior 'binding' of the multiplication sign, and can be performed with the aid of a 'stack' and instructions which affect only the top one or two objects on the stack, thus:

Instruction, leading to ...	Stack ('top' on the right)
Take 3	3
Take 5	3 5
Multiply	15
Take 7	15 7
Take 11	15 7 11
Multiply	15 77
Add	92

The instructions in this form can be abbreviated to the following:

$$3 \quad 5 \quad \times \quad 7 \quad 11 \quad \times \quad + \qquad \text{(B1)}$$

which is a transformation of (A1). A corresponding transformation of

$$(3 \times 5 + 7) \times 11 \qquad \text{(A2)}$$

would be

$$3 \quad 5 \quad \times \quad 7 \quad + \quad 11 \quad \times \qquad \text{(B2)}$$

As can be seen in these examples, and can be proved in general (see Section 7.1.1), the B-forms are unambiguous in spite of the fact that they contain no brackets. They are the reverse Polish notation forms equivalent to the standard notation A-forms.

Reverse Polish is based on an ⟨operand⟩⟨operand⟩⟨operator⟩, or post-fixed operator structure; direct Polish is based in a similar way

23

c

on prefixed operators — ⟨operator⟩⟨operand⟩⟨operand⟩ — and in
our examples would give

$$+ \quad \times \quad 3 \quad 5 \quad \times \quad 7 \quad 11 \tag{C1}$$
$$\times \quad + \quad \times \quad 3 \quad 5 \quad 7 \quad 11 \tag{C2}$$

The first of these may be read *sum(prod(3,5),prod(7,11))*, but, like the
inverse Polish forms, they are unambiguous without any need for
brackets.

The diagram in Figure 1a is instructive, as it shows the vocabulary
elements in direct Polish order when projected on the left and read
downwards, but normal order when projected vertically. A topology
preserving transformation of the figure gives Figure 1b, which shows
reverse Polish order when projected on the left and read upwards.

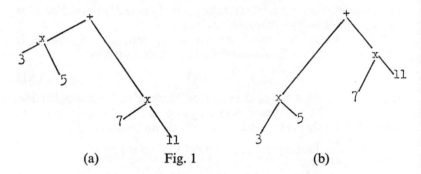

(a)   Fig. 1   (b)

Since the order of the items in reverse Polish is the order in which
they have to be considered for manipulation, it will be apparent that
the transformation to reverse Polish (suitably generalised) is implicit
in every process of compilation. So far as algebraic expressions are
concerned, the following algorithm achieves this transformation:

Z: Read next item to A
    if A holds an object, output it and **go to** Z **else**
    if it holds a closing bracket **then** unload the stack till the opening
        bracket is met, abolish both and **go to** Z **else**
Y: **if** it binds more tightly than the item on the top of the stack, or
      is an opening bracket **then** place it on the top of the stack and
      go to Z **else**
    output the operator on top of the stack and **go to** Y

and a wide range of syntactic structures can be compiled by suitable
further elaboration of this algorithm.

5

THEORY OF NAMES

Basically, what in Section 2.7 we called an 'object' is what in algebra is called a 'variable', and its name is the letter used in referring to it. In parallel with this we may think of the object as a location in computer storage and its name as the address of that location. But the interaction between these two viewpoints is such that the basic concept needs to be reviewed critically from several angles. In doing this it will be a good thing to try to reach a unified theory covering names which do not refer to variables as well.

5.1 Names and codewords

The first problem arises out of temporary working space for recursively used routines. Each time the routine is entered, a new and independent working area will be required, without abandoning what has already been raised. Dijkstra has coined the happy phrase 'simultaneous *incarnations* of the routine' to describe this situation. What it implies here is that a letter, used to name a working variable of a routine, may have several store locations reserved for it, although all but one of these are very much 'in reserve' at any one time. This shows that, depending on how we handle simultaneous incarnations, it is more or less essential to keep the ideas of the name in the language and the address in the store independent of one another.

Further, when a name is introduced into a mathematical formalism, it is introduced with certain implied properties. We begin with 'let x be . . .'. These properties are lost if a name becomes transformed simply into an address. If we restore this information we arrive at (a slight generalization of) what Iliffe (1961, 1962) calls a *codeword*. This we may define as follows

A codeword is an E-object which contains the address of another E-object together with information as to how the contents of this E-object are to be interpreted.

To avoid giving a false impression of Iliffe's own use of the word, it should be added that the second E-object may be composite (a list) and in this case an important part of the information is the number of components, and how to select the *nth* one. Note, too, that compiled machine code is an E-object, and that the above definition does not prevent a codeword from containing the equivalent of a label or of a routine name, or even of a piece of machine code constructed during the running of the programme.

An important distinction is made in algebra between 'bound' and 'free' variables in the context of certain constructions. Within such a construction the free variables have the same meaning as they do outside it, but bound variables are completely internal to it, and are dummies in the sense that any other letters will do just as well (excluding such as would lead to confusion). They arise in two ways. (1) In a context like

$$\int_0^\infty e^{-tx}.f(x)dx$$

the letter x could be replaced by any other (except t or f) without affecting the meaning of the expression in any context in which it might be written. (2) In a definition of a function such as

$$\ldots \text{ where } g(x) = a.\sin(px+q)$$

the letter x is again a dummy. Computationally these two cases are very different. In the first, x is almost certainly the name of an object created temporarily to assist in the evaluation of the function; in this case it is an object of the same sort as t, and in computational usage it is described not as a bound variable but as a local variable. (Thus a local variable is a piece of explicitly named temporary working space.) In the second case the x is due to be replaced by something more significant whenever the definition is applied. It is called a *formal parameter*, the expression which replaces it during an actual call being referred to as an *actual parameter*. In one sense, therefore, it has no real existence and no storage will ever be required for it. But an alternative point of view could be that it is an object whose value is another name — that of the actual parameter, although this concept still needs further study if it is to cover the case in which the actual parameter is an expression which is not a variable, as in $g(t^2+2)$. Alternative approaches here are (1) that an expression can be a value, and (2) that the value must be an implicit label. On the codeword side the implication is that among the alternative interpretation-cues available there must be two, one of which allows the value found at the address in the codeword corresponding to the formal parameter to be another codeword, and the second of which allows the value of the latter to be a piece of machine code which is to be obeyed in order to obtain the implicit value of the former. The words *argument* and *operand* are both used synonymously with *parameter* and *bound variable* by some writers. The suggested 'name whose value is a name' shows a close relationship between parameters and indirect addressing.

26

5.2 Lambda notation

Church (1941) introduced a notation for the definition of functions in which the symbol λ plays a special part; in this notation the above definition of $g(x)$ is written

$$g = \lambda(x)[a.\sin(px+q)]$$

and instead of $g(t^2+2)$ one can write

$$\lambda(x)[a.\sin(px+q)](t^2+2)$$

That is, λ is followed by two or three further syntactic units; first there is a list of bound variables, then an expression involving these variables (the *body* of the λ-expression). If we stop at this point, we have a 'function divorced from any operands', such as '*sin*' or 'the Bessel function J_2'. But this may be followed by a list of actual operands; in this case we have the result of applying the function to these operands.

For an alternative notation for implying use of parameters see Section 8.

5.2.1 Recursive functions in lambda-notation

There is no *obvious* difficulty in applying λ-notation to recursive definitions; for example, we can write

$$\text{Sum} = \lambda(x,y).\textbf{if } y = 0 \textbf{ then } x \textbf{ else } \text{Sum}(S(x),P(y))$$

in place of the form given in Section 3.2. But Landin (1964), in his work on the semantics of CPL and other languages, prefers to follow Curry (1958) and make the following further transformation in this case. By a second dose of λ-notation all recursive references are removed from *inside* the definition

$$\text{Sum} = [\lambda f.\lambda(x,y).\textbf{if } y = 0 \textbf{ then } x \textbf{ else } f(S(x),P(y))](\text{Sum})$$

and then the definiand is removed altogether from the right hand side by assuming the existence of an operator Y such that if F is a function, then YF is the solution of $x = F(x)$.

$$\text{Sum} = Y\lambda f.\lambda(x,y).\textbf{if } y=0 \textbf{ then } x \textbf{ else } f(S(x),P(y))$$

Now in this definition f is a bound variable being 'solved for and found to have' the value *Sum*; it can be replaced by *Sum* or by anything else, but to replace it by anything else would be rather foolish. So we write

$$\text{Sum} = Y\lambda\text{Sum}.\lambda(x,y).\textbf{if } y =0 \textbf{ then } x \textbf{ else } \text{Sum}(S(x),P(y))$$

And if this seems to be back where we started, then we must point out that what $Y\lambda$ achieves is (a) to remove all suspicion of circularity, and (b) to remove all doubt as to the propriety of ascribing the same meaning to a variable occurring bound inside and free outside the expression in which it is bound. This transformation has influenced the

27

way in which recursively defined routines are handled in CPL; it would appear to be the origin of the somewhat retrograde step (Dijkstra, 1963) of *requiring* recursive routines to be explicitly declared as such by the prefix *rec*, instead of *permitting* a routine to be declared non-recursive when this will permit more efficient translation.

5.3 Assignment as an all-purpose imperative

The effect of Church's notation is that definition of a function is brought under the form of an assignment statement (the '=' is imperative). And by implication, *g* is an object whose value is $\lambda(x)[a.sin(px+q)]$ in spite of the fact that it is not a variable in the algebraic sense. It is a type of object whose value is, in a sense, its meaning, in which it also resembles the variable whose value is an expression. One result of this is that the concepts of 'literal', 'constant' and 'variable' which we shall shortly discuss must be held to apply to functions as well as to any other sort of value.

In view of the way computers work, it would not be surprising if statements in a 'primitive' language, such as might suffice for definition of formal semantics (Section 7.6), were all assignment statements; it is therefore gratifying to observe that *go-to* statements can also be brought under this form by assuming the existence of a special variable called **control**, whose value does not remain constant, but points continually to the 'active spot' in a programme. To explore this, consider a particular case of the programme quoted in Section 1.1, namely,

$$x := 1; \quad y := 1; \quad k := 1;$$
$$Q: \ x := kx+1; \quad y := ky; \quad k := k+1;$$
$$\text{if } y < 100 \text{ then go to } Q; \quad e := y/x$$

We could rewrite this in several ways out of which we choose the following only because it best illustrates the points we want to make.

$$x := 1; \quad y := 1; \quad k := 1; \quad z_1 := S;$$
$$z_2 := \textbf{control}; \quad x := kx+1; \quad y := ky; \quad k := k+1;$$
$$R: \textbf{control} := \text{if } y < 100 \text{ then } z_2 \text{ else } z_1;$$
$$S: \qquad e := y/x$$

Note that alternative forms for the statement labelled R are

R1: **if** $y < 100$ **then control** $:= z_2$;
R2: **control** $:=$ **if** $y < 100$ **then** z_2 **else** S;
R3: i $:=$ **if** $y < 100$ **then** 2 **else** 1;   **control** $:= z_i$;

and that using either R1 or R2, the statement $z_1 := S$ is unnecessary.

5.4 Implications of assignment

As a second method of approaching the subject, consider what

28

happens when we simulate this programme manually. What we do is to write out something like

x:	1		2		5		16		65		326
y:		1		1		2		6		24		120
k:			1		2		3		4		5		6
e:													2.717

it being understood that in each line whenever a value is inserted the previous one is crossed out. Now most languages require the complete form of a programme to begin with the equivalent of 'let x, y, and k be integers. . . ' . Many computers are so organized as to deal differently with integers and with numbers which may contain a fractional part (rational approximations to real numbers); indeed the latter often require a greater storage space than the former. So 'let x . . .' becomes an indication to the computer to allocate an appropriate amount of storage and to associate the letters x, y . . with the storage so allocated. This corresponds fairly closely to our action in putting these letters as the 'titles' to successive lines, but since computers are relatively less efficient at searching and association than we are, and since their storage locations are all numbered (with addresses), the compiler usually makes a transformation in the programme equivalent to

1: line4 := 1;   line5 :=1;   line6 :=1;
2: line4 := line4.line6 + 1;   line5 := line5.line6;
    line6 :=line6+1;
3: if line5 < 100 then go to line2; stop;
4: 1   2   ⎫ etc, inserted during running
5:   1   1   ⎬ of programme
6:     1   ⎭

Note that optionally the compiler can render line 3 as

3: if integer in line5 < 100 then go to instruction in line2;

it is now combining information about the nature of the contents of the addresses with the addresses themselves; in other words it is adopting something nearer the codeword approach. If x and y were bound variables something more elaborate would be required; possibly line4 might be preloaded with 'use line27' or something to that effect. However, it is much more satisfactory if line3 can read 'if integer whose address is in line5 . . .'

But having once introduced the inside of the computer, we can make a third approach. For this purpose let us suppose that ':=' is but one of many symbols of the general form '?='. Then x ?= y is only valid if x refers to an object (is sited), and its effect is to change the value of that object — the various forms changing it in different ways. What can it change it to? Possibilities, not all applicable in every context, are

1. The literal 'y'. E.g. after $x\ ?= cat$, the value of x is a string of three letters, c, a, t, copied from the string in the instruction and belonging uniquely to x.
2. The name of the literal 'y' in the programme. E.g. if $x\ ?= cat$ is stored in locations 50–54, then the value of x becomes '52–54', or some equivalent like 52(3) (meaning three characters starting in location 52).
3. The name of a unique literal 'y' elsewhere in the programme. This, with minor variation only, must be what happens at '$z_1 := S$' in the illustration programme.
4. The value of the object of which 'y' is the name. This is the usual interpretation by which, after $y := 2; x := y;$ the value of x is 2.
5. The name (inside the computer as an address) of the object whose name (outside the machine, in the programme) is 'y'. (I.e. the codeword for 'y'.)
6. In case the value of y should be a name (as it will be if it was assigned by a $?=$ of type 5), the value of the object whose name is the value of y. This is a form of indirect addressing, and as the result may be another codeword, we must add
7. As (6) but 'fully transparent', continuing until a value which is not a codeword is reached.

These seven possibilities apply when the right-hand side of an assignment statement is a single name, and they are not exhaustive, because we still have not considered complications such as names which have λ-expressions as their values. But the right-hand side may be an expression containing several names, in which case the possibilities apply to them independently. This shows that the '$?=$' notation has served its usefulness in directing our thoughts, and must now be abandoned. Also options (6) and (7) apply equally (with slight modification) to the left-hand side — another pointer in the same direction.

It is tempting to argue that 'what goes on inside the computer' ought to be eliminated from the semantics of a good programming language, but it is not quite as simple as that; the computer in the abstract serves as a model of the semantics of the language (cf. Gilmore, 1963). For example, we can clarify the semantics of a possible instruction of the form 'let x mean y' by saying that it involves $x\ ?= y$ in sense (5), with all subsequent references to x in the context $z := \ldots x. \ldots$ bearing interpretation (6) so far as x is concerned; the value of x becomes the codeword for y and subsequent calls for x yield the value currently associated with the codeword which is the current value of x. The peculiarity required of the subsequent calls need not be compiled into them, it can be the result of including a suitable mark in the information part of the codeword at the time when it is assigned to x as its value — a mark which says to the world at large 'treat me as transparent'.

5.5 Literals

A constant is an object whose value never changes. In the written language advantage can be taken of this to use its value as its name; it is then called a literal.

It is unfortunate that letters are usually not literals whereas numbers are, but this is due to the fact that x usually stands for a number whereas 12 is 'literally' 12. Consider the character π. This is conventionally a constant with the value 3.14159 . . . and therefore not a literal. Convention can be broken in either direction. Greek scholars, or mathematicians who want their results in algebraic form, will require it to be a literal; conversely one can use π as a variable just as one does x or any other letter.

Within a machine the address of an object is unlikely to be its value, and a rather different concept of a literal is required — if, indeed, there is much use for it at all. Since an address is an integer, many machines permit some economy in storage by making available instructions of the form 'add the number n' as well as of the form 'add the contents of address n', but this is so restricted a 'literal' usage that it may well have to be ignored during compilation and introduced later during an optimization process. (Option (2) in the interpretation of '?=' is a somewhat similar device; its main virtue is that it saves copying when circumstances permit such an economy.) In a more general way, whenever a value is stored within the programme and subject to the 'write-protection' which guarantees pure procedures against accidental alteration, then there is some point in referring to it as a literal.

If the same literal occurs at several places in a programme (as, for example, '1' in '$x := x+1;\ \ y := y+1$'), each occurrence can 'be itself', though some compilers in fact prefer to regard them all as names of a single external value, probably because it facilitates a standard treatment. (All codewords will require the same storage space, and the variable element, which is the length of the literal itself, is taken outside the programme.) But this is not so of other constants. A constant, unless system defined (as π might well be), must occur as a literal once in a programme, at that point where it is defined, and other uses must name the object which is in the definition. This is outstandingly true of labels, and hardly less so of definitions of procedures, etc. An awkward fact is that one of the 'other' uses can easily occur before the 'defining' one; compiler writers are all too familiar with the various ways of getting over the difficulties this gives rise to.

5.5.1 Notation for literals

In natural languages, quotes are used to mark the distinctions we have been discussing, but the usage is not entirely consistent, and the only universal rule is that surrounding a character string in

31

quotes signals a departure from the interpretation which would otherwise be in force. Usually in programming languages it converts the contents of the quote from non-literal to literal. This is the same as the usage in English by which

Jack is singular

means that a certain boy (whose name is 'Jack' and who is, in a sense, the value of this name) is rather odd, whereas

'Jack' is singular

means that the four-letter string is (a noun which has the property of being) singular. But English can also provide precedents for the converse usage. Thus we may write any one of the following sentences:

1. He was elevated to the chair.
2. He was 'elevated' to the chair.
3. He was literally elevated to the chair.

Where (1) is neutral in tone, in (3) any metaphoric usage in (1) is removed — i.e. he not merely went up to a superior position in the hierarchy but was caused to go up physically in space. But in (2) the effect of the quotes may be either the same as that of 'literally' in (3), or may be precisely the opposite, making it sarcastic (he was removed to a place where he could no longer be a nuisance) and even less literal. The pitfalls of trying to ignore the distinction altogether can be seen in a sentence such as

Jack is a noun, and is a conjunction.

A further complication arises from the fact that early computational work was numerical; this has given rise to the convention that sequences of numerals are literals even without quotes. But then, perversely, many languages which adopt this convention break it by allowing integers as labels. In Algol, compiler writers have gone on strike over this point, and have generally refused to implement integer labels. The issue became acute in Algol because it was the first language to combine bound variables of label type with call by name (actual parameters not being reduced to a value before entering the procedure) with the result that in an actual parameter list a situation could arise in which it was not clear from the immediate context whether an integer was a literal or a name.

5.6 A formal theory of names

It will be clear from all this that there is as yet no received theory of names, although there is a great need of one. What follows is merely a sketch which tries to avoid both the less necessary constraints and the more grievous traps.

One fairly clear-cut approach is suggested by a paper of Gilmore (1963), and although it generalizes his presentation somewhat, we

32

take the liberty of applying his name to it, and defining a Gilmore system as one in which

1. Any string of characters is eligible to be a name. Names may be valid, invalid or intrinsic.
2. Each name has (potentially) an intermediate value and a final value.
3. A result is the final value of a 'programme' — i.e. of a character string supplied to a machine for interpretation as a name.
4. Rules exist by which certain names are assigned immediate final values — e.g. there are rules for determining that a string is a literal.
5. A definition is a subsequence of a programme whose semantics is that a certain literal is the final value of a certain name.
6. For names to which a final value cannot be assigned in either of the above ways, there are rules for transforming a string into its intermediate value. The result of this transformation is a sequence of names of which one is an operator and the remainder are operands. (There are some degenerate cases. Note that it is the transformation rules which distinguish when a name is eligible to be an operator.)
7. There are rules by which the result of operating by any operator on appropriate final values as operands can be evaluated.
8. When the final value of a name is not immediate (under (4) or (5)) it is recursively defined as being the result obtained by applying the operator to the final values of its operands.
9. A name is valid when the application of the rules leads to a final value. An intrinsic name is one which has no value but is permitted under (6) and (7) as an operator. All other names are invalid. The set of all valid names under a given set of rules is a language.
10. Note that when the programme is in a Polish notation the transformation under (6) consists merely of splitting the string into substrings; in other cases it may be more complicated. In a language using λ – calculus, a name whose final value (however derived) is a λ-expression without parameters ranks as an operator.

But this approach as it stands applies only to function languages. Something more, bringing in the external world more explicitly, and relating names to codewords, is required in general.

We therefore define a value as a string of characters held at an address in store. Input and output values are included by a suitably wide definition of store, and the notion of address includes that of a sequence of addresses to accommodate values of various lengths. A programme is a particular example of a value once it is in the machine. There is a pre-grammar whose function is to divide any string of characters into 'words'. It may be trivial — e.g. 'spaces separate

33

words' — but it is also flexible and can alter its interpretation according to circumstances — e.g. it might first determine whether certain conditions hold under which the rule is that 'full stops separate words'. However, one invariable rule is that from an opening quote to its mating closing quote is indivisible. This rule is tempered by the fact that the value on which the pre-grammar is called upon to operate can begin inside outer quotes.

There is a dictionary, which is in (at least) two parts, a system part and a part which can be added to or subtracted from by a programme (if several programmes are running at once each has its own second part). The dictionary consists of a 'lexicon' or series of 'entries' (character string plus associated material) and a 'rubric' or set of rules for applying the lexicon. The function of a dictionary is 'to record the interpretation of words', and in our case the dictionary may record that a word

(a) is an intrinsic name, and provide details of the effect of using it as an operator, or
(b) is a sited name, and provide means for obtaining its codeword.

The second of these is deliberately a little vague to allow room for alternative ways of handling, e.g. a name which refers to the top of a push-down list or stack, some of which might involve a short calculation to obtain the codeword. The first might also provide a codeword to a section of programme. If a word is not 'found' in the dictionary, the rubric may invoke the pre-grammar to split the name and re-enter the dictionary recursively. (This provision allows for such features as subscripted names.) Any word which can neither be found nor analysed is treated as a literal — this will usually be the case with strings of numerals.

One of the most difficult aspects of this approach is that it requires generalization of the concept of evaluation. There is a sense in which it is fair to call 'it will produce 2.717 as the value of e' an evaluation of the programme in Section 5.3. I.e. the number is the value of e, but its production is the outcome of the evaluation of the programme; evaluation is a process which, applied to imperative strings, means obeying them, with results that are important but do not include the assignment of a value to the string. In generalizing the Gilmore system to include procedure languages it is necessary to permit the process of evaluation to include such operations as adding to and taking from the dictionary (both lexicon and rubric, in general) together with the storage allocation actions which these operations imply.

This problem is the same as is dealt with by Landin (1965, Pt. II), and it also arises in the use of the word 'evaluation' by Ross (1962; see Section 15.4). Here we are concerned primarily with the nature of a 'name'; the theory as we have sketched it is thought to be complete and sound at an abstract level, but to call for much work on, for example, how to keep the rubrics consistent. Interpretations which cannot be brought within its scope run considerable risk of running into trouble through inadequate definition of the relation between the names of the language and the codewords which correspond to them in the external world.

6

SYSTEMS ASPECTS

English is English whether spoken by a soprano or by a bass, with an American or British accent, and a poem is the same poem whether printed in a large and sumptuous library edition or a small-print paper-back. One may ask how far differences of this sort are permissible in programming languages. In fact, there is considerable divergence between what the various programming languages will tolerate in this respect.

The normal input to a computer is either 80-column punched cards or punched paper tape. A large computer will have both. The former has twelve rows, and therefore twelve punching positions per column, whereas the latter has five, six, seven or eight punching positions across the tape. In theory, therefore, alphabets ranging from 2^5 ($= 32$) to 2^{12} ($= 4096$) characters are in use, but in practice, cards used this way are rarely punched with more than three holes per column, while on the smaller paper tapes some characters are reserved for functions similar to the 'shift lock' and 'shift release' of the typewriter, so that alphabets of between forty and eighty characters have been the rule. Alongside any computer installation there will be separate equipment which can read cards or tape and produce therefrom paper printed with normal alphabetic and other signs, colloquially known as 'hard copy' (or as 'listed copy' — a shibboleth for detecting the card user). In the case of card equipment, one card produces one line of print made up of eighty characters; from tape each character corresponds, as it were, to pressing one key of a typewriter (shift keys counting as separate depressions). A line of hard copy from tape is thus whatever occurs between one 'carriage return' symbol and the next; it is of no particular length, and the number of tape characters is only loosely related to the number of characters (including blanks) on the hard copy, since the former includes shifts. However, a line longer than the width of the paper will not produce a satisfactory hard copy, and any paper tape which is to produce good hard copy must be divided into lines less than a certain maximum which can conveniently be put at eighty characters. With this convention the distinction between card and tape practice effectively disappears.

It should be added that until the I.S.O. standard character set becomes effective, the situation is complicated by the fact that differ- ent codes are in use by different equipments, which do not agree even on shifts and carriage returns, so that tape produced by one yields gibberish, often overrunning margins, on another. Neverthe- less, a computer ought to be able, by means of a 'dictionary program- me', to accept any code, and should not be prevented from doing so by premature interpretation of any punching as a control symbol.

It is becoming an acknowledged principle of 'good practice' that what matters is the appearance of the hard copy — produced, of course, on an appropriate equipment. This was not always so. In many systems using Autocode, for example, if 3.14159 were punched with an unnecessary figure shift in the middle (which of course would not show on the hard copy) it would be rejected as improperly punched. One result of accepting the principle is that if a programme is printed in a book like this, and a tape punched and its hard copy checked against the book as correct, then the tape is a good one. In some languages facsimiles of the hard copy are preferable because in true print (and some modern typewriters) the characters are not all the same width, so that there is no guarantee that characters on suc- cessive lines which are vertically aligned are, in fact, on the same column of the cards they represent. This is a tiresome complication in languages where it is important, and one may hope that future languages will avoid it.

6.1 Semantics of layout
Where languages differ considerably is in the semantic or gram- matical content of page layout. In natural languages it is usual to distinguish units known as words, separated by spaces. A new line is equivalent to a space unless precautions are taken against this; otherwise, in prose at least, a new line has neither semantic nor grammatical content. There is, however, a vague semantic content in the paragraph. In natural languages grammatical analysis often takes place with 'semantic reinforcement' (See sections 2.2, 15.3 and 15.4), and such vague semantic implications can have a significance not required in languages with less ambiguous grammars. Neverthe- less, page layout is sometimes pressed into service. Algol dispenses with it altogether; neither space nor newline symbols convey anything whatever and they are, from another point of view, noise symbols, though they are normally used to provide that redundancy which human beings like and computers prefer to be without. (Cf. Dickens (1837)). Languages at the autocode level usually demand one instruc- tion per line; that is, the newline character has the semantic function of sentence separator.

Cobol, which in some respects prides itself on a relative freedom of expression, has certain very rigid format requirements in the matter of page layout. The first six characters in a line constitute a line number (and line numbers if present must be in ascending sequence but not necessarily consecutive) or they may be blank; the seventh is either blank or contains a hyphen to indicate that a word has been 'run over' from the previous line; the next word (or part word if hyphenated in Col.7) begins either in the 8th or the 12th space, according to whether it starts a new paragraph (or section) or not. In some parts of the programme successive further indentations by four spaces at a time may be used in certain circumstances to improve readability. Once the main contents of a line have been begun, freedom comes back, and, for example, any 'run' of several spaces is linguistically equivalent to a single space. This system of line numbering is presumably also the reason why the new standard Fortran sets the maximum line length at seventy-two characters.

A system need not be confined to a single language, and when it is not, then some commonality of layout is desirable. The M.I.T. 'Project MAC' is an example (Corbato, 1963). ('MAC' is a multiple acronym. As 'Multiple Access Computer' it refers to the development (from the principle of time-sharing a machine between programmes) that each user can have his own input/output organ in his own office. In other expansions ('Man/Machine Aided/Assisted Computation/Cognition') it refers to programmes which allow the machine to help the inexperienced user by 'conversing' with him). In MAC the unit is the 'document' or 'file', which consists of lines numbered as we have described. A new document is typed in under the control of a system programme which provides the line numbers — going up in hundreds — and thereafter accepts anything it is given other than an *immediate* new line. The latter allows the controlling programme to switch to other modes in which, say, the line numbers are under the control of the user for making insertions (off the even hundreds) or corrections, or for actually doing things with a document that has been typed in. The 'conversation' principle applies in that the machine will type 'wait' and later 'ready' if called upon to do something that takes an appreciable time and cannot be interrupted. The immediate hard copy is therefore a record of the combined activities of user and machine. The machine can be asked to print a fair copy of any document it holds; it will do this with line numbers, in case the purpose is to see exactly how it stands before revising it. The name of the file is a two-part name of which the second part specifies the language (with 'data' as one option). A request to the machine to 'Compile Trajectory-Algol' will result in the creation of another file with the name 'Trajectory-Machine-code' provided that the file 'Trajectory-Algol' actually exists; if difficulties are met because the latter is ungrammatical, its line numbers will be used to pinpoint the trouble in reporting it to the user.

Thus line-numbers, which were originally card-numbers introduced as an insurance against the accident of a pack of cards getting out of order, have their continuing uses in system operations, and such as to make it worth including them even on tape-punched originals. They form a left-hand marginal annotation to any document carrying them, and this annotation is sufficient, possibly together with signing-on and signing-off routines like titles and ENDs, to cover the requirements of a system which has to handle many languages without doing violence to the internal conventions of any of them.

A system of the sort we have been describing inevitably poses the question whether languages can be mixed — to state a more specific case, whether an Algol programme might call a subroutine already present in the machine but in Fortran, for example. As a general question this must be considered to be beyond the scope of this book, but those interested could consider the problems involved by noting the explanations given later of the different ways in which parameters are called in the two languages mentioned. The general problem may be expected to be greatly clarified by further work on formal semantics (see Section 7.6).

6.2 Traps

Next we must consider the implications on a language of being used within a system that is capable of interfering. This includes the subject of 'traps'. The earliest computers did what they were told, however absurd, and produced some sort of answer, however unrealistic, unless they got into a loop. The cautious programmer would see that before asking for x/y say, he inserted an order **if** $y = 0$ **then go to** . . . , thereby wasting time and space in 99 % of the times it was executed. In most cases there was nothing he could do but stop, so later machines saved him the trouble by stopping for him. But then attention focussed on the cases when there was something he could do, and the outcome of this was the trap, which we can define as a jump instruction not in the programme but imposed by the hardware as a result of certain conditions arising, and made in such a way as to preserve all information necessary to return to the interrupted programme at the point from which the jump was made.

There are two rather different implications of the trap for the designer of programming languages. First, the writer of the programme does not know when the trap will occur, and must therefore give *advance* instructions as to what to do if and when it does occur. Secondly, the programmer is no longer writing a self-contained story, in terms of quantities solely of his own choosing and naming; he has to take account of things not of his own creation, and therefore with names not of his own invention. Actually the latter is a wider matter than traps, since the same comment applies to items like console switches, but these have played little part in language development because until the advent of time-shared machines their

D

use by programmers was deprecated more and more as computer time became more and more expensive.

If a programmer does not anticipate a trap, it will usually lead into a system routine which reports its nature and terminates the programme. The earliest trap-like feature in a high-level language was probably in Mercury Autocode, where 'label 100' was a system routine unless set in the user's programme, and was invoked in case of overflow, diversion by zero, etc. A more developed use of the concept came in Cobol, but it was ignored in Algol (unless incorporated in procedures in machine code). It is perhaps worth noticing that the concept of a trap is best allowed to be level independent; that is, it may be a feature of the hardware of the machine, but the high-level programmer really has no need to know whether this is so or whether it happens as a result of the way his programme is compiled.

6.3 System programming

System routines are generally lengthy or involved enough to encourage the development of higher-level languages in which to write them, but they are also highly machine dependent. Consequently, although languages have been developed for this purpose, they none of them have the generality of interest which warrants dissemination, and rather regretfully no further mention of such languages will be made.

7

FORMAL LANGUAGE STRUCTURE

We use the phrase 'formal language structure' to cover two subjects, formal grammar and formal semantics. The former was initiated by Chomsky (1956 and 1959) and has led to a veritable explosion of work; the latter, in any strict sense of the word 'formal' is almost unexplored territory, but includes such of the theory of compiler writing as has been formalised. The most widely understood item in this field is the development from Chomsky's notation due to Backus (1959) and used in the Algol report edited by Naur (1960), often called Backus Normal Form or Backus-Naur Form (Knuth 1964B). In this work we shall use the abbreviation CBNF to cover any notational form which can claim to belong to this family. For a number of reasons we confine our attention to the linguistic approach and ignore the considerable body of related work in the theory of automata.

7.1 Basic principles of formal grammar

Chomsky initiated the mathematical study of grammatical structure by the following abstraction. A grammar, on his definition, consists of two vocabularies and a set of 'productions'. One vocabulary is the vocabulary as we already know it, from which the language is constructed; this is the *terminal* vocabulary. The other, or *non-terminal* vocabulary, consists of the names of structural units. The two are distinguished by using lower-case letters for the former and upper-case letters for the latter. The *productions* are permissive replacement rules. One of the non-terminal symbols, usually denoted by S, has a unique status. The language consists of all terminal strings which can be obtained by suitable choice of productions from S.

The very simple grammar

$$S \rightarrow AB$$
$$A \rightarrow a$$
$$A \rightarrow ac \qquad \text{Language 1}$$
$$B \rightarrow b$$
$$B \rightarrow cb$$

leaves one no choice but that S must be replaced by AB, but then allows two alternatives in each case for replacing A and B, both of which result in eliminating non-terminal symbols with the result that this grammar permits just the four derivations

1. $S \rightarrow AB \rightarrow aB \rightarrow ab$
2. $S \rightarrow AB \rightarrow aB \rightarrow acb$
3. $S \rightarrow AB \rightarrow acB \rightarrow acb$
4. $S \rightarrow AB \rightarrow acB \rightarrow accb$

Note that

$$S \rightarrow AB \rightarrow Ab \rightarrow ab$$

is equivalent to (1), because it differs only in the order of performance of independent substitutions. On the other hand, (2) and (3), which both lead to *acb*, are different. By incorporating a notation to indicate the derivation they may be written

$$[ac][b] \quad \text{and} \quad [a][cb]$$
$$A \quad B \qquad\qquad A \quad B$$

respectively. In this language the string *acb* is ambiguous, with two interpretations depending on whether *c* is assumed to be derived from *A* or *B*. (Note that the expanded forms may be regarded as being in a metalanguage —Language 1a— related to the original one by a simple modification of its replacement rules. Not every grammar can be so modified, but context-free grammars (see below) always can.)

The grammar

$$S \rightarrow aT$$
$$T \rightarrow bT \qquad\qquad \text{Language 2}$$
$$T \rightarrow c$$

includes a recursive production, and can lead to strings of any length, viz., to *ac*, *abc*, *abbc*, *abbbc* ..., which we can write as $ab^n c$ ($n \geqslant 0$).

Backus and Naur, by introducing the metalinguistic symbols $\langle, \rangle$ and $|$, made it possible for the non-terminal vocabulary to be more helpful. (They also replaced $\rightarrow$ by $::=$, the sole (but real) merit of which seems to be that this symbol is unlikely ever to occur in the terminal vocabulary of any language.) The metalinguistic brackets allow the capital letters of Chomsky to be replaced by descriptive words or phrases, so that, for example, instead of $S \rightarrow AB$, we can write

$$\langle \text{sentence} \rangle ::= \langle \text{subject} \rangle \langle \text{predicate} \rangle$$

The third symbol is a metalinguistic 'or else', which allows us to compress Language 1 into

$$S ::= AB$$
$$A ::= a \,|\, ac$$
$$B ::= b \,|\, cb$$

In an interesting formalism due to Chomsky and Schutzenberger

42

(1963) this symbol is replaced by '+', leading to

$$S = (a+ac)(b+cb) = ab+2acb+accb$$

When this formalism is used, any coefficient greater than unity implies ambiguity in the language.

It is not clear whether Chomsky intended his terminal symbols to be quasi-numerical (i.e. literal) or quasi-algebraic (i.e. nominal), but Floyd (1963) has made this distinction explicit by introducing a third element of vocabulary for which he uses Greek letters; this is 'representative' vocabulary, consisting of symbols whose replacement rules confine them to replacement by a single terminal character. Examples of representative symbols are λ for $\langle$letter$\rangle$, and ν for $\langle$numeral$\rangle$; formally they rank as terminals at least so long as the sets they represent do not overlap.

7.1.1 Illustrations

As immediate applications of these concepts we may note first that $S = a+SbS$ and $S = a+bSS$ express the grammar of mathematical expressions (a) with infixed operators and (b) with prefixed operators, if a is representative of simple operands and b of operators, and that expansion of these (by repeated substitution of the right-hand side into itself) confirms earlier statements about their ambiguity.

Secondly, the ambiguity in Language 1 is precisely that which we noted in the sentence 'John's hates work' in Section 2.2, where interpretation depends on whether 'hates' belongs to the subject or to the predicate. It is interesting to note that the ab form in this example is valid — 'Your hates are ineffective; John's work!' — but that the $accb$ form runs foul of the agreement-in-number which English demands — contrast 'John's fish fish flounder' (presumably John's fish are large and carnivorous!). Another interesting feature of this example is that in natural languages a principle of style would seem to rule that an ambiguity of this sort may be resolved when possible by choosing the structure which matches that of a previous sentence. No such principle has so far been invoked in any programming language.

Similarly, if b is effectively a representative symbol, Language 2 reproduces the structure of the sentences in 'The house that Jack built'. We have only to set

$$a = \text{This is the}$$
$$b = \langle\text{noun}\rangle \text{ that } \langle\text{verb}\rangle \text{ the}$$
$$c = \text{house that Jack built}$$

to see in a general way how it works (obviously a more accurate analysis is possible by going into greater detail).

7.2 Further developments

Recently, Iverson (1964) has suggested a notation which achieves a compromise between the verboseness of Backus and the uninforma-tive anonymity of Chomsky. Basically this consists in listing the non-terminal vocabulary in a three-column table, the columns being (a) line number, (b) Backus left-hand side, and (c) a right-hand side in which the line numbers and not the Backus forms are used. It also in-corporates further higher-level features in addition to the Backus vertical line, but these are not altogether felicitous and have been supplemented and modified by Burkhardt (1965). Burkhardt quite rightly makes a sharp distinction between the symbols of the langu-age being described and those of the metalanguage, but his method (using heavy type for the former) has its own disadvantages. He also fails to appreciate the value of the 'representative' concept, which Iverson distinguishes by means of letters instead of line numbers. The following grammar illustrates most of the features involved:

a	letter	a|b|c|d|e|f|g| etc	Language 3
d	numeral	0|1|2|3|4|5|6|7|8|9	
e	empty		
s	sign	+| −	
1	identifier	a|*{a|d}	
2	integer	$1 d	
3	number	{s|e}{2|$0 d.$1 d}↑1{$_{10}${s|e}2}	
4	primary	1|3|(7)	
5	factor	4|*↑4	
6	term	5|*{×|/|÷}5	
7	expression	{s|e}6|*s6	

Here black type has been suppressed in the representatives. The asterisk indicates the thing being defined and thus shows the oc-currence of simple recursion of the sort in Language 2. Braces are metalinguistic brackets. Thus the last item indicates that an expres-sion is a term preceded by either a sign or nothing, or is an expression followed by a sign and a term. The sequence is deliberately arranged so that occurrence of a number higher than the one currently being defined implies a more elaborate recursion, as in the definition of a primary as an identifier, a number, or any expression enclosed in brackets. The ↑ in 'factor' is the exponentiation sign. The ↑ and $ in 'number' (and elsewhere) are Burkhardt's additional metasymbols; in words, this definition reads

a number is an optional sign ('sign' or 'empty') followed by either an integer or 'at least no digits "point" at least one digit' followed by at most one . . . (exponent part).

Note that 'at most one' is equivalent to 'optional', and other synony-mous constructions of this sort can be found; this is an inevitable result of introducing higher-level features. The value of a specific notation for 'at most' appears in dealing with languages like Fortran,

44

where, for example, names are restricted to six letters in length.

Language 3 was constructed by adapting a part of the syntax of Algol. Note first that a term *can* be a factor, which *can* be a primary, and that an expression can be a term but can also be an expression followed by + or − and a term. So

$$35$$
$$x$$
$$x - 35$$
$$x - 35 + k$$

are all possible expressions, and in the last $x - 35$ is an expression and k a term; we cannot misunderstand and think that $35 + k$ is an expression to be subtracted from x, because the grammar provides no option that way round. But a primary can be an expression in brackets, so that

$$x - (35 + k)$$

is possible. Similarly, $-a \uparrow 2 + b/c$ is defined by the grammar to mean $-(a \uparrow 2) + (b/c)$, and not, for example, $(((-a) \uparrow 2) + b)/c$. Thus this syntax controls the interpretation of algebraic expressions (or such of them as involve no further symbols or notation) of any length and complexity. At least, it does so in so far as it is unambiguous, but in fact it has been badly constructed, since although it provides only one analysis for $-a \uparrow 2$, it provides two for $-3 \uparrow 2$. It is a very simple but useful exercise to revise this grammar to remove this ambiguity.

7.3 Context-free and other grammars

Chomsky showed that within his basic concept, four nesting categories of language could be distinguished, with corresponding nesting types of grammar. In the outermost, which he called Type 0, production rules are very free, permitting, for example, replacements like

(a) aAb D → aHD   i.e. AbC → H in the context a ... D
(b)   PQ → QP

Such grammars he showed rather despondently to be (a) so free as to be of little use, and yet (b) not free enough to characterize natural languages. His Type 1, or *phrase structure* grammars, restricted productions to those in which a single non-terminal was replaced by a non-null string; this banned all rules which *shorten* a string to which they are applied, but a rule like (b) above, though technically banned, may be retained as a mere shorthand for the permitted sequence

$$PQ \to PZ \to QZ \to QP$$

where Z is a new non-terminal used only in these three rules. In Type 2, or *context-free* grammars, the single non-terminal must stand by itself on the left-hand side of a production, i.e. the replacement must be freely available in any context. In Type 3, or *one-sided linear* grammars, only rules of the form

$$A \to a \quad \text{or} \quad A \to aB \quad (B \neq A)$$

are allowed. It is important to realize that 'context-free' has become a technical term with the meaning defined above, and may not be used with the freedom of natural English.

A language, defined as a set of terminal strings, may be produced by several grammars, and these may differ in ways which may or may not be trivial for a given purpose. (1) The replacement of one rule by three as above, while theoretically interesting, is a needless complication in practice. In a similar way we can show that a rule $A \to acB$ is only a technical violation of the Type 3 restrictions, whereas a right-hand side with more than one non-terminal would violate them fundamentally. (2) Gorn (1963) cites the language $a^m b^n$ $(m+n>0)$ to show the effect of choice of grammar on presence or absence of ambiguity. It is generated by either of

1. $S \to a|b|aS|Sb$ 2. $S \to ABAB$
$A \to a|aA$
$B \to b|bB$

If a and b are representatives for ⟨adjective⟩ and ⟨noun⟩, then (1) permits 'binary electronic coder decoder' to be interpreted in six ways, including ways like 'binary electronic-coder decoder'; whereas (2) insists on 'binary and electronic, coder and decoder'.

A language is said to be *decidable* under a given grammar if it is possible to write an algorithm which will determine whether any arbitrary string of its terminal characters is in the language or not; in practice this will probably mean to display at least one derivation of the string or to prove that none can exist. (E.g. it is not difficult to prove that no string of a's, b's and c's beginning with b or c can belong to Language 2.) One virtue of the Type 1 restriction is that it makes it possible in theory to write down *all* the strings *of a given length* in the language; this restriction is therefore sufficient to make a language decidable. On the other hand, if the insertion of ⟨empty⟩ between any two characters may open up new vistas, life is clearly going to be very difficult, and in fact it can be shown that there are undecidable languages. In practice, it is much more important to have an efficient 'parsing' algorithm; one, that is, which will lead quickly to a structural analysis in the majority of cases. More recent study of grammars has aimed at isolating features which will help this.

7.4 Pseudo-context-free languages
First, however, let us return to the fact that natural languages transcend phrase structure grammars. Chomsky wrote of the need in

natural languages for study of 'transformational grammars', in which changes more cataclysmic than replacements can occur (cf. changes from active to passive, or direct to reported speech, without change of meaning). We can mention three ways in which even the higher *programming* languages show features outside those of context-free languages.

The first of these may be described as the introduction of lambda-notation into the metalanguage. Consider the language defined by

$$S \to \Lambda B.BB.C$$
$$C \to DE$$
$$D \to x \mid xD$$
$$E \to y \mid yE$$

where Λ is a λ-operator which may not take effect until C has become a terminal string. Clearly $C \Rightarrow \rangle x^{\,m}y^n$ and $S \Rightarrow \rangle x^m y^n x^m y^n$, where the symbol '$\Rightarrow \rangle$' implies 'by way of one *or more* productions'. Had we written $S \to CC$ or $S \to DEDE$, there would have been no control over the equality of alternate exponents, and it is a fact that this control cannot be achieved by a context-free grammar in the Chomsky sense, although our notation achieves it without violating the 'single-symbol left-hand-side' concept. The ability to specify identical choice of replacements for two or more occurrences of the same non-terminal is a definite requirement. Cobol grammarians have introduced a notation for it (Section 10.3). Rose (1964) has modified the 'definable sets' of Ginsberg and Rice (1962) (which are equivalent to context-free grammars) in a similar direction in his 'extended definable sets'.

Secondly, natural languages permit a greater semantic control of syntax than a CBNF system admits. The ambiguity in

The driver of a lorry that is full of gin . . .

can be semantically resolved (on the basis of the *meanings* of 'driver' and of 'lorry') if 'that' is replaced by either 'who' or 'which'. A similar situation occurred in Algol over the construction

if B then C else D = E

which would be (if *B* then *C* else *D*) = *E* if *C* was of type integer or real, but if *B* then *C* else (*D* = *E*) if *C* was of type boolean. Since *C* could be a formal parameter, it might be impossible to determine the choice until run-time. This ambiguity was removed in the 1962 revisions; an obviously sound change taking the short view but more dubious on the long view, since it may have been the first appearance of a challenge which will eventually have to be met.

Meanwhile, there is an alternative way of regarding this overlap between syntax and semantics, for that is what we are dealing with. It appears most sharply defined in the matter of declarations in Algol

47

and similar languages. The Algol syntax contains the following productions among many others

⟨variable identifier⟩ ::= ⟨identifier⟩
⟨simple variable⟩ ::= ⟨variable identifier⟩
⟨type list⟩ ::= ⟨simple variable⟩|⟨simple variable⟩, ⟨type list⟩
⟨type⟩ ::= **real**|**integer**|**boolean**
⟨type declaration⟩ ::= ⟨type⟩⟨type list⟩

The last three of these define, straightforwardly, the structure of a type declaration, but the first two are nonsense except that they imply that ⟨identifier⟩ could be written instead of ⟨simple variable⟩ on the right-hand side of the third. This is because they are trying to say something which the notation cannot convey, namely, that a simple variable is an identifier which has occurred in a type declaration. What is required is that the third production should be revised to read ⟨identifier⟩ instead of ⟨simple variable⟩ and that the first two should be cut. This will create a gap, since ⟨simple variable⟩ is used elsewhere in the syntax. Means to bridge this gap must be supplied by a means of saying that, because of the semantics of a declaration, the gap will be bridged at compile time by converting the type declaration into a temporary production in which ⟨simple variable⟩ may be any of the identifiers in the type declaration. On this view, which is substantially identical with that put forward by Caracciolo di Forino (1963), there are two levels of Chomsky-grammar in Algol, an outer or formal grammar whose terminals are the characters used in Algol, and an inner, or semi-semantic grammar, whose terminal vocabulary consists of identifiers (phrases to the outer grammar) and whose productions must be provided as part of the programme. Declarations are rules to the inner grammar but phrases to the outer one. Alternatively, one may replace ⟨simple variable⟩ by ⟨identifier⟩ throughout, and leave it to the semantics to say that certain strings are grammatically correct but meaningless. There are precedents in natural languages, both for grammatically correct nonsense (e.g. 'the corner of the round table') and for defining one's proposed usage as one goes. A third solution may lie in the more adequate development of formal semantics (see Section 7.6.1)

Both the inner and outer grammars of Algol are context-free but the combination is not. The standard demonstration (Floyd, 1962) that Algol is not context-free rests on the 'programme'

begin real xx. . . ; xx. . . := xx. . . **end**

which is valid Algol if all the *xx*. . . 's are of equal length, but otherwise either invalid or grammatically correct nonsense according to your point of view. (At this level we overlook the fact that *xx*. . . is void in this programme, and concentrate on the fact that it must be sited.)

48

7.5 Simplifying properties of grammars

We pass now from the point of view of the 'speaker' who uses a grammar to synthesize sentences, to that of the 'hearer' who uses it to analyse them and extract a meaning. Much of the work on formal grammars has been aimed at determining the properties which make them easy to analyse without robbing them of their power. For the sake of brevity we summarize this work more or less in the form of a glossary of the terms which have been used.

The simplest grammars are *polynomial* (because the Chomsky-Schutzenberger expansion terminates). An example of one is given in Section 9.3.

Next come *one-sided linear* grammars, the Type 3 grammars, linear because no term in the expansion ever contains more than one non-terminal. They are not as narrow as might appear, for Chomsky showed that every Type 2 grammar can be revised into Type 3 unless it proves impossible to eliminate productions of the form $A \Longrightarrow \phi A \psi$ (neither ϕ nor ψ empty), when the grammar is described as *self-embedding*. (This may well have some bearing on the differences between the 'horrible' sentences of Section 3.3.) But since this condition bans the algebraic use of brackets, it is too restrictive for most purposes. A language is described as *metalinear* if it contains a production $A \to BC$ which cannot be eliminated, but B and C themselves give rise to linear (or metalinear) productions which do not interfere with each other.

Within context-free languages, Ginsberg and Rose (1963) distinguished a grammar as *reducible* if some non-terminal other than S gives rise to a proper subset of the productions, and as *sequential* if the non-terminal vocabulary can be arranged in order, starting with S, in such a way that *each* member defines a subset of the grammar defined by its predecessors — i.e. if in Iverson-Burkhardt notation no definition contains a line number greater than its own.

Floyd (1963) defined an *operator grammar* as one in which no two non-terminals ever occur on the right-hand side of a production without a terminal between them. In such a language it is sometimes possible, for any pair of terminals occurring consecutively (possibly with a non-terminal between them), to say which emerged first in the derivation. A grammar in which it is always possible to do this he called a *precedence grammar*. Broadly speaking, an operator which emerges earlier in a derivation has a stronger 'binding power' — one can see this in Language 3 — but Floyd's concept is more powerful than that of binding power because it transcends the implications of the fact that binding power is a scalar quantity.

Floyd (1964) has also shown that in some context-free grammars the ultimate origin of a terminal symbol can be deduced from a consideration of a limited number of its neighbouring terminals. These he calls *bounded-context* grammars. (Note that 'context' here refers to the terminal string, whereas it is the non-terminal which gave rise to it whose replacement is context-free.)

7.6 Formal semantics

All the above features can be shown to contribute something to the problem of creating an efficient parsing algorithm for a language. As soon as we transcend context-free grammars, the situation becomes more dominated by the practicalities of compiler writing, and we propose at this point to introduce the idea of formal semantics. In many areas to which languages are applied, a strictly formal semantics is impossible. This is because semantics concerns relations with a qualitatively different external world. Since the external world of programming is of the same nature as language itself, the situation here would seem to be different; nevertheless very little work in the nature of formal semantics has yet been done.

A 'Gilmore system' as defined in Section 5.6 is a formal semantic once the rules there referred to are supplied. But Gilmore's approach applies only to function languages and our attempted extension is hardly adequate for semantic purposes.

Consider also a new machine for which no compilers have as yet been written. To write a compiler for a language on this machine is to define what the machine will do in response to any valid sentence in the language, and thus the compiler *is* the semantics *vis-á-vis* this machine. To write a programme which can transform a suitably expressed description of the language into a compiler is therefore to turn the description into a formal semantic of a sort — but only of a sort unless we can eliminate *'vis-á-vis* this machine'. One answer to this is to design a formal machine with only such instructions as may be regarded as the 'primitives' of formal semantics. Any inefficiency in such a machine would be as irrelevant as is the inefficiency of the definition of *sum* in Section 3.2. Currently, however, this approach has been limited to practical work in compiler writing in which efficiency on a particular machine has been of overriding importance. Pioneer work in this direction is the Syntax-directed Compiler of Irons (1961 and 1963), the Sequential Formula Translator of Samelson and Bauer (1960), the Compiler-compiler of Brooker (1963), and the work of Huskey (1961).

Two features characterize all the work in this field. (1) The input language is a transformation of CBNF augmented to supply semantic material, and (2) the productions are ordered in a definite sequence for consideration, and ambiguities are removed by accepting the first successful parse which is found (thus defining, by the ordering of the productions, which possible meaning of an ambiguous string is to be *the* meaning).

7.6.1 An example

Let us return to Algol declarations for illustration. We first revise the syntax of identifiers to read

$\langle$id tail$\rangle$ ::= {$\langle$letter$\rangle$|$\langle$numeral$\rangle$}{$\langle$id tail$\rangle$|$\langle$empty$\rangle$}
$\langle$identifier$\rangle$ ::= $\langle$letter$\rangle\langle$id tail$\rangle$|$\langle$letter$\rangle$

We do this because a production such as

$\langle$identifier$\rangle$ ::= $\langle$letter$\rangle$|$\langle$identifier$\rangle${$\langle$letter$\rangle$|$\langle$numeral$\rangle$}

contains two traps. (a) It invites the compiler to accept an initial letter as the complete identifier in accordance with the second principle of the previous paragraph. (b) In trying the second alternative, the compiler will get into a tight loop by asking whether we have an identifier (defined as an identifier (defined as . . .))? However, $\langle$letter$\rangle$ $0{\langle$letter$\rangle$|$\langle$numeral$\rangle$} is an acceptable alternative.

We now reinterpret each production in the following way. A pointer indicates a certain character in the string being analysed. A production $\langle$K$\rangle$ ::= . . . becomes a logical function with a side-effect, namely the function K? which, if it is possible to find a $\langle$K$\rangle$ beginning with the character indicated by the pointer, takes the value **true** and moves the pointer to the character following this $\langle$K$\rangle$, but takes the value **false** and leaves the pointer unmoved otherwise. The routine K? is built up out of the routines corresponding to the items on the right-hand side of the production for $\langle$K$\rangle$. In simple cases the transformation is obvious; thus the alternative form for $\langle$identifier$\rangle$ at the end of the previous paragraph becomes

logical function identifier?
    if letter? **then go to** P;
    identifier? := **false**;   go to exit;
P: **if** letter? **then go to** P;   **if** numeral? **then go to** P;
    identifier? := **true**;
exit:

Unfortunately, not all the potential sequences of a developed CBNF notation can be dealt with quite so mechanically — note even here the care which has gone into line *P*, which would advance the pointer correctly *even if the classes* $\langle$letter$\rangle$ *and* $\langle$numeral$\rangle$ *are not mutually exclusive*. Nevertheless the principle is clear, and *S*? is a decision algorithm for determining whether a string belongs to the language or not.

Next we make use of the fact that a compiler is almost bound to follow this same procedure but to interpolate further actions as it goes through the motions. Thus the above recognition procedure for an identifier will be expanded into a compilation procedure something like

logical function identifier?
    raise storage for an identifier on the stack;
    if letter? **then go to** PP;
    identifier? := **false**;   cancel storage;   **go to** exit;

51

PP: put letter in store;
P: **if** letter? **then begin** AL: add letter to store; **go to** P **end**;
if numeral? **then begin** AN: add numeral to store; **go to** P
end;
identifier? := **true**;
exit:

and these additions can be formalized by corresponding additions to
the production (omitting those which may be taken for granted)
thus:

⟨identifier⟩ ::= ⟨letter⟩⟨PP⟩ \$0{⟨letter⟩⟨AL⟩|⟨numeral⟩⟨AN⟩}

the insertions being compiled in, as further logical functions which
always have the value **true**. With this sort of notation the Algol
declaration situation can be dealt with by maintaining lists of
declared identifiers and putting the semantics into the syntax thus:

⟨declaration⟩ ::= ⟨type⟩⟨remember type as T⟩⟨type list⟩
⟨type list⟩ ::= ⟨identifier⟩⟨add it to T-list⟩{,*|e}
⟨simp var⟩ ::= ⟨identifier⟩⟨check that it is on one of the T-lists⟩

The third of these productions is now no longer a meaningless redundancy. (Nor, come to that, can it any longer be compiled 'as a
logical procedure whose value is *always* **true**' — in which there may
be a moral somewhere.)

7.6.2 Other treatments

The above treatment follows fairly closely to that of Leavenworth
(1964), which we have adopted because it fits most closely into a
unified formalism. Leavenworth also sets out to show that both the
recognition and the semantic routines can be written in Fortran —
and though he fails signally to show that this is a happy choice, it is
something to show that the semantics can be defined in so machine-
independent a way in principle.

The treatment of Irons was the reverse of the above both in notation (a relatively trivial matter) and in method (more important).
Where we would write

⟨primary⟩ ::= ⟨letter⟩|etc,
⟨exp⟩ ::= ⟨primary⟩|⟨exp⟩⟨sign⟩⟨primary⟩

he would have

letter → primary {LDA $-\rho_1$}
primary → exp {ρ_1 }
exp sign primary → exp {ρ_1 ;STA $-$ t; ρ_3[t←ti]; ρ_2-t}

the items in braces being the semantics, and dependent on the machine
being compiled for. This particular set would cause an input string
$A+B$ to be subjected to the following transformations:

52

letter(A)+B
primary(LDA–A)+B
exp(LDA–A)+B
exp(LDA–A) sign(ADD) B
exp(LDA–A) sign(ADD) letter(B)
exp(LDA–A) sign(ADD) primary(LDA–B)
exp(LDA–B; STA–t; LDA–A; ADD–t)

Each syntactic item has an associated string, that is, and the object is to convert a series of items to a single item, merging their strings according to the rules in braces, where $\rho_1, \rho_2 \ldots$ are the 'parameter' strings counting outwards from the arrow (i.e. right to left). The reversed arrow in the square brackets implies that in copying ρ_3 every t is to be replaced by ti (thus generating t, ti, tii, .. as temporary working stores). The final string is the machine assembly code which will leave the value of $A+B$ in the accumulator ('load accumulator from B; store accumulator into t; etc'). Had the string been $A+B+C$, the t's derived from $A+B$ would have become modified in the final transformation which would have given

exp(LDA–C; STA–t; LDA–B; STA–ti; LDA–A; ADD–ti; ADD–t)

This is inefficient coding, but Irons show that by adding redundant syntactical forms with short-cut interpretations, such as

$$\text{exp sign letter} \rightarrow \text{exp } \{\rho_3 \; ; \rho_2 \; - \; \rho_1\}$$

the coding can be made efficient. (It would also need modifying from the above to accommodate the Algol rule as to the order of evaluation of primaries.) Provision is also made for generating labels and for error monitoring. The Algol declaration situation is dealt with by a double pass, the first one generating additional syntactic rules.

The Compiler-compiler starts along the same general lines, with its own variations in layout, but it is much more difficult in the published accounts to disentangle what is machine independent. Mention should also be made of Gargoyle — 'a language for compiler writing' (Garwick, 1964).

Griffiths and Petrick (1965) have studied the efficiency of various sequences of attack on the recognition problem. A given parse may be expressed in the form of a tree with S at the top and the terminal string along the bottom. One may try to build this tree from top to bottom or from bottom to top. For certain types of grammar these are practically equivalent, but when they are not, the latter is generally the more efficient. Both modes, but particularly the latter, become more efficient if explicit notice is taken of which terminals cannot possibly start the derivation from a given non-terminal. Judged by these criteria the Irons scheme receives very high marks. The ultimate aim in formal semantics must be a descriptive system which combines theoretical impeccability with prospects of efficiency in compilation.

Somewhat different approaches have been made by Landin (1964, 1965), McCarthy (1963), and Ross (1962, 1964). Landin's work effectively lays bare one possible set of 'primitives'. The approach of the Cambridge CPL team has been that a functional language based on lists, λ-calculus, McCarthy-type conditionals (see Section 12.1) and certain arithmetic primitives (such as $sum(x,y)$) can be made to express with precision all one wants to do in computing, and that the structures of 'popular languages' are just 'syntactic sugar' over this 'semantic centre'. Thus the semantics of any language can be accurately specified by stating to what applicative expression any given construction in the language is equivalent. Certainly, in one case where Algol interpretation has tied itself up in knots — the recursive use of **own** — Landin's approach clarifies what it is reasonable to expect the interpretation to be and how the concept might be revised with advantage.

McCarthy's aim has been to go somewhat deeper and investigate formal methods of determining when different computational procedures are equivalent in the sense that they must produce the same result — e.g. a recursive and an iterative solution of the same problem. Ross's approach is more in the main tradition but being based on the requirements of natural languages it permits semantics to influence syntactic analysis, and claims that most of its resources are untapped by any programming language. It is discussed further in Section15.4.

8

MACROGENERATOR

Most programming languages show remarkable complication as soon as one looks at them closely. It will be advantageous to consider first one which is simple enough to survey fairly fully and show how it exemplifies the principles we have set out.

Macrogenerator (Strachey, 1965) is a function language which enables the user to write in abbreviated form anything which involves considerable repetition of certain patterns, even though the repetition is with variations too elaborate to permit simple use of 'ditto'. We shall call the language in which the patterns occur the *pattern-language*. A repeated pattern such as we have described can be given a name by writing

$$\text{§DEF,}\langle\text{name}\rangle,\text{``}\langle\text{pattern in full}\rangle\text{''}; \qquad (A)$$

where $\langle\ \rangle$ retain the metalinguistic significance they have throughout the rest of this book, and " " are used where Strachey would in fact use our metalinguistic brackets. (The quotes in (A) may be omitted if they serve no useful function, but are necessary if, for example, the pattern contains a semicolon.) The variable parts in the full pattern are represented by $\sim$1, $\sim$2. ., read as 'parameter No.1', etc, and the abbreviated form for the pattern is then

$$\text{§}\langle\text{name}\rangle,\langle\sim1\rangle,\langle\sim2\rangle\ldots; \qquad (B)$$

where $\langle\sim n\rangle$ indicates the string which is to be substituted for $\sim n$ on this occasion of use. In serious use the pattern-language is probably a machine assembly code — the affinities with Irons' semantic items are obvious — but the Macrogenerator makes no assumptions at all about it except that it does not use unpaired quote symbols, and at the end of this section (sub-section 8.4) we show it in action on three nursery songs in English; the first of these shows a completely straightforward application.

From the function language point of view, the structure $\text{§}X,A,B,C;$ is equivalent to the structure $X(A,B,C)$ of more conventional mathematical notation, and except when X is DEF it may be read as 'function X of A, B and C'. It is important to realize that (A) and (B) above are identical in syntactic structure but differ in semantics; we shall refer to them indifferently as functional forms but shall differentiate them as definitions and abbreviations respectively when it is

55

necessary to do so. Functional forms may be nested, and when a definition is nested this usually corresponds in conventional mathematical notation to the usage ' . . . *where* . . . *is* . . . ' . For example §*A*,*B*,§*DEF*,*A*,"*Q*~1";*;* is '*A*(*B*) *where A*(*x*) *is Qx*'.

8.1 Syntax

In Backus style, which usually gives the panoramic view before the detail, the formal syntax can be expressed thus:

1. ⟨complete text⟩ ::= ⟨text⟩⟨endsymbol⟩
2.   ⟨text⟩ ::= ⟨text unit⟩|⟨text unit⟩⟨text⟩
3.   ⟨text unit⟩ ::= ⟨quote⟩|⟨function⟩|⟨opentext⟩
4.   ⟨quote⟩ ::= "⟨text⟩"

although this is slightly restricting — see below —

5.   ⟨function⟩ ::= ⟨function head⟩⟨function tail⟩
6. ⟨function head⟩ ::= §⟨item⟩
7.   ⟨function tail⟩ ::= ;|,⟨item⟩⟨function tail⟩
8.   ⟨item⟩ ::= ⟨unit⟩|⟨unit⟩⟨item⟩
9.   ⟨unit⟩ ::= ⟨quote⟩|⟨function⟩|⟨plain text⟩
10.   ⟨open text⟩ ::= ⟨character⟩|⟨character⟩⟨open text⟩
11.   ⟨plain text⟩ ::= ⟨plain ch.⟩|⟨plain ch.⟩⟨plain text⟩
12.   ⟨character⟩ ::= ⟨any character from the set available to the equipment except §, " or ".⟩
13.   ⟨plain ch.⟩ ::= ⟨any ⟨character⟩ except , or ;⟩
14.   ⟨endsymbol⟩ ::= "

Although these productions suffice to analyse a message, they do not guarantee a semantically meaningful one; in particular, the distinction between definitions and abbreviations is ignored, and the parameter notation. Productions 1, 2 and 3 amount to the statement that a complete text consists of a string of open texts, quotes and functional forms terminated by an end symbol. Productions 4, 12 and 13 show that opening and closing quotes are always paired, and that an unpaired closing quote can only arise from production 14. Since productions 2, 3 and 4 are recursive, quotes can be nested, so that the end of a message will be detected by monitoring when 'depth in quotes goes negative'. Productions 5, 6 and 7 define a function as

$$§⟨item⟩;$$
$$or \quad §⟨item⟩, . . . ⟨item⟩;$$

so that § . . . ;, like the quote symbols, have the quality of brackets. Within these brackets, unless further protected by quotes, the comma has a special significance and the semicolon cannot be introduced. An ⟨open text⟩ is simply a sequence of characters not enclosed in either type of bracket, and a ⟨plain text⟩ fulfils the same role under conditions in which the special interpretation of the comma and semicolon must be applied. Production 4 requires the contents of a quote to conform to the syntax of the language as a whole, and in particular inhibits it from containing an unmatched §, an unnecessary restriction which we shall remove in considering the semantics.

8.2 Semantics

Let us next consider the semantics informally. It is semantically *useless* to write a definition which is not used, or parameters in excess of the number required (except for **where** definitions), but *meaningless* to write a functional form with a first ⟨item⟩ which has not been defined or with an inadequate number of parameters; the former are merely silly but the latter, although not syntactically incorrect according to the above productions, should give rise to error monitoring.

To interpret a string in this language the ⟨complete text⟩ is dealt with unit by unit. An ⟨open text⟩ is copied to the final form as it stands, and a ⟨quote⟩ likewise. In copying a quote, the quote symbols that surround it are omitted, but any within it are retained, and also any commas, §, or other symbols which might otherwise have a special interpretation. If a functional form is met, it is interpreted. A temporary copy is made, each ⟨item⟩ being copied according to the same rules as before. This can involve recursive interpretation. When this is complete, the definition of the first ⟨item⟩ (as interpreted, if this differs from the original form) is sought, *the search starting with the most recently acquired definitions.* Unless this is DEF or one of the other 'machine macros' described below, the final copy is made from the second ⟨item⟩ in the definition, copying it *according to the usual rules* (with recursive interpretation if necessary) but with the additional rule that *parameters are substituted for literally* from the corresponding ⟨item⟩ of the temporary copy (literally because they have already undergone interpretation). If the first ⟨item⟩ is DEF, the functional form is interpreted by adding its second and third items to the list of definitions. When interpretation is complete, the temporary copy, including all definitions to which it may have given rise by the interpretation of its parameters, is deleted. (If any definitions arose out of the final copy, these are retained.)

Formalizing these semantics gives rise to some interesting points. It becomes apparent that the definition strings must be regarded as in different languages at different stages! We adopt a compromise notation which retains Backus brackets within an Iverson-Burkhardt framework for syntax and uses square brackets for semantic items. We assume the existence of a push-down list of strings and we use the abbreviation [*] to mean 'concatenate the current symbol with the string on the top of the list'. Then in broad outline, but it seems impossible to fill in further detail, the formal semantics can be written

57

$\langle\text{text}\rangle ::= \$0\{\langle l\rangle[*]|\langle n\rangle[*]|\langle c\rangle[*]|\langle\text{outerquote}\rangle|\langle\text{function}\rangle\}$
$\{\langle\text{endsymbol}\rangle[\text{stop}]\}$
$\langle\text{outerquote}\rangle ::= \text{``}\$0\{\langle l\rangle[*]|\langle n\rangle[*]|\langle c\rangle[*]|\S[*]|\langle\text{innerquote}\rangle\}\text{''}$
$\langle\text{innerquote}\rangle ::= \text{``}[*]\$0\{\langle l\rangle[*]|\langle n\rangle[*]|\langle c\rangle[*]|\S[*]|\langle\text{innerquote}\rangle\}\text{''}[*]$
$\langle\text{function}\rangle ::= \S[\text{pushdown}]\langle\text{item}\rangle\ \$0\ \{,[\text{replace}]\langle\text{item}\rangle\};[\text{apply}]$
$\langle\text{item}\rangle ::= \$0\{\langle l\rangle[*]|\langle n\rangle[*]|\langle\text{outerquote}\rangle|\langle\text{function}\rangle\}$

where $\langle c\rangle$ is 'comma or semicolon', $\langle n\rangle$ is 'numeral', and $\langle l\rangle$ is any other character but these and § and quotes. As long as one meets symbols in the $\langle l\rangle$, $\langle n\rangle$ or $\langle c\rangle$ classes, that is, one copies them [*] on to the end of the string; failing this one investigates the possibility of a quote, a function, or the endsymbol. The distinction between $\langle\text{outerquote}\rangle$ and $\langle\text{innerquote}\rangle$ is solely in the absence of the copy sign after the first and last symbols of the former. Immediately on finding a function sign one pushes down the current list and starts a new one; this is the temporary copy. In doing so, one must replace the inter-item commas by some new symbol because others without this status may be uncovered from quotes. On reaching a semicolon which is not a part of an included item (and an item cannot begin with a semi-colon) one performs 'apply'.

Now 'apply' consists in removing the temporary copy from the push-down list, allowing the previous top to emerge, and adding the interpretation of the temporary copy to it. It is here that one feels that the lack of detail is regrettable, nevertheless, three things make it difficult (though probably not impossible) to incorporate further detail into the main formalism. (1) Most of the definitions have been supplied dynamically, so that we have a situation similar to the 'Algol declaration' one. (2) The machine macros, DEF, etc, have to be treated differently. This is part of the third, which is (3) the syntax of the definition strings now differs from that of the input message at least in respect of the character $\sim$.

The resolution of all these points involves revolutionary developments which go beyond the scope of the present work, and may indeed be showing a way into transformational grammars. But a glimpse may be obtained by considering the following revision of the grammar given above.

1. $\langle\text{open text}\rangle ::= \$0\{\langle\text{textunit}\rangle|\langle\text{int.ch}\rangle[\text{error}]\}\text{''}[\text{stop}]$
The only novelty here is the inclusion of a monitor. This induction (it has rather exceeded the notion of a production) means 'carry out the process of looking for a text unit, alternatively (if that fails) look for an internal character and signal an error; repeat this as often as you can, or, when you can no longer do either, then find a closing quote and stop' (This does not prevent [error] from calling halt.)

2. $\langle\text{text unit}\rangle ::= \text{``}\langle\text{quote}\rangle\text{''}|\ \S\langle\text{function}\rangle|\langle\text{ext.ch not}\rangle\text{''}[*]$
3. $\langle\text{function}\rangle ::= [\text{pushdown}]\langle\text{item}\rangle\$0\{,[\text{replace}]\langle\text{item}\rangle\};$
$[\text{replace}]\ [\text{apply}]$

4. ⟨quote⟩ ::= $0{"[*]⟨quote⟩"[*]|⟨not"⟩[*]}
5. ⟨item⟩ ::= $0{"⟨quote⟩"| §⟨function⟩|⟨not, or;⟩[*]}

These have been rearranged in the interests of efficiency; thus (2) will usually amount to 'not an opening quote? not a §? not an internal character or a closing quote? then copy'. One result is to eliminate the separate inner and outer quotes. Replacement of the comma will be by the internal character #. Now we add

6. ⟨definition⟩ ::= $0{~{⟨n⟩[trans]⟨parameter⟩| [error]}|⟨text unit⟩}#[pop up]
7. ⟨parameter⟩ ::= $0{⟨any ch except#⟩[*]}#[pop up]

which will be called by [apply]. (6) means 'look for something beginning with ~ or for a text unit, the former followed by a numeral or there is an error, but having found the numeral transfer the nth item of the temporary copy to the input (pushing down the true input)'. The⟨parameter⟩which is then expected is, of course, found and treated according to (7), but *only because* [trans] put it there; it was not there in the original string!

8.3 Further details of the language

The second of the nursery songs in the next section is slightly more complicated than the first, having two levels of repetitiveness, and consequently a little nesting of functional forms; it is not difficult to apply the above rules to follow through the interpretation. The third, with two solutions, one by myself and one by the Cambridge research student who checked my solution on the machine—is more like an exercise in structural analysis than a convenient method of abbreviating, but it illustrates a number of points which we cannot spare space to describe in detail. These include

1. Careful control of the 'depth in quotes' of the ~ sign, to determine at which copy it is uncovered, and hence interpreted; this, when definitions are nested, determines whether $~n$ refers to the parameters of the inner or the outer function. (It solves the 'nonlocal variable which is a formal parameter of an outer procedure' problem.)
2. The functions S, P, W which are the 'successor' 'predecessor' and 'word' functions respectively on the numerals.
3. The introduction of 'variable functions' whose names depend on a parameter, as in §$VERSES~1$.
4. The use of (3) combined with the rule that definitions are sought beginning with the most recently acquired, to control the 'exit' from a recursive definition, since

$$§~1, §DEF, ~1, " \ldots ";, §DEF, X, " \ldots ";;$$

will behave differently when $~1$ is X from how it will behave when they are not the same.

59

5. Various features in connection with lay-out control.

In addition to DEF, the complete Macrogenerator contains a number of other 'machine macros'; these are all late additions to improve the fluency in directions where it was felt to be desirable. A function UPDATE revises an existing definition, where DEF would either override it only temporarily or else waste extra storage space overriding it permanently. A function §VAL,X; allows the defining string of X to be copied without interpretation; in simple cases which do not involve interpretation it is equivalent to §X;. There are also functions to permit arithmetic and radix conversion on numerical strings. To illustrate UPDATE, the functional form §AORB; will output alternately A and B if defined with the aid of a subsidiary function Q thus:

$$\S\text{DEF},Q,A;\S\text{DEF},\text{AORB},\langle\S\S Q;;\rangle,\S\text{DEF},A,\langle A\S\text{UPDATE},Q,B;\rangle;,$$
$$\S\text{DEF},B,\langle B\S\text{UPDATE},Q,A;\rangle;;$$

One noteworthy property of Macrogenerator is that it is a counter-example to any notion that one can always make do with a single type of bracket, since it shows that a sequence like

$$\langle\ldots(\ldots)\ldots\langle\ldots)\ldots\rangle$$

may sometimes be both possible and significant, namely, when the semantics depends on the depths in the two forms of bracket independently. The one serious inability of the Macrogenerator in its complete form would seem to be that if the pattern-language includes quote symbols, then it is impossible to derive any part of the interior of an output quote by means of a functional form. To provide this facility, either one must admit distinct metaquotes, or one must add a character which, I have argued elsewhere (Higman, 1963), is a necessary part of any completely self-handling language, namely, **c** (read as 'the character'), which encloses the immediately following single character in implicit 'super quotes' — even if this is **c** itself.

8.4 Examples

On the facing page we reproduce in facsimile the examples already referred to. They were prepared on a Flexowriter (a typewriter incorporating a paper tape punch and reader), and the paper tape fed into the computer. The output tapes to which this gave rise were fed into the reader of the Flexowriter and produced the copy, all but a few lines of which is reproduced on the three following pages. (Note: (1) the local convention which allows the new line and space symbols occurring between *→ and →* to be suppressed, and (2) that the ***Z is a system code signifying the end of the tape.)

60

```
1. §DEE,VERSE,<
Old Macdonald had a farm, E-I-E-I-O,
And on this farm he had some ~1, E-I-E-I-O!
With a ~2 ~2 here and a ~2 ~2 there,
Here a ~2 there a ~2 everywhere a ~2 ~2,
Old Macdonald had a farm, E-I-E-I-O.
>;
§VERSE,chicks,cheep;
§VERSE,ducks,quack;
§VERSE,turkeys,gobble;
  etc., etc.,
```

COMPUTER
INPUT

```
2. SONG FROM A CHILDREN'S GAME
§DEF,VERSE,<~1~1
Hey do diddledy ho ~1
>;
§DEF,LINE,<
The ~1 wants a ~2>;
§DEF,FORM,<§VERSE,§LINE,~1,~2;;>;
§FORM,farmer,wife;
§FORM,wife,child;
§FORM,child,dog;
§VERSE,
We all pat the dog;


§DEF,S,<§1,2,3,4,5,6,7,8,9,§DEF,1,<~>~1;;>;
§DEF,P,<§N,0,1,2,3,4,5,6,7,8,§DEF,N,<~>~1;;>;
§DEF,W,<§L,One,Two,Three,Four,Five,Six,Seven,Eight,Nine,§DEF,L,<~>~1;;>;
§DEF,HEAD,<
§W,~1; men went to mow, went to mow a meadow,
>;
3. §DEF,END,<
One man and his dog, went to mow a meadow>;
§DEF,TAIL,<§W,~1; men,  §~1,§DEF,~1,<§TAIL,§P,>~1<;;>;§DEF,6,<
§TAIL,5;>;§DEF,2,<§END;>;;>;
§DEF,VERSE,<
§HEAD,~1;§TAIL,~1;>;
One man went to mow, went to mow a meadow,§END;
§REST,2,§DEF,REST,<§VERSE,~1;§~1,
§DEF,~1,<.§REST,§S,>~1<;;>;§DEF,9,<!>;;>;;


§DEF,VERSES,<§VERSES~1,§DEF,VERSES~1,<§VERSES,§P,>~1<;;>;
§DEF,VERSES1,4.  ALTERNATIVE METHOD;;§VERSE,~1;>;
§DEF,W,<§L,One man,Two men,Three men,Four men,Five men,Six men,*→
     →*Seven men,Eight men,Nine men,§DEF,L,<~>~1;;>;
§DEF,HEAD,<
§W,~1; went to mow,went to mow a meadow>;
§DEF,REST,<§REST~1,§DEF,REST~1,<§W,>~1<;
§REST,§P,>~1<;;>;§DEF,REST1,<One man and his dog,went to mow a meadow>;;>;
§DEF,VERSE,<
§HEAD,~1;
§REST,~1;>;
§VERSES,9;
>
***Z
```

COMPUTER OUTPUT

1.

Old Macdonald had a farm, E-I-E-I-O,
And on this farm he had some chicks, E-I-E-I-O!
With a cheep cheep here and a cheep cheep there,
Here a cheep there a cheep everywhere a cheep cheep,
Old Macdonald had a farm, E-I-E-I-O.

Old Macdonald had a farm, E-I-E-I-O,
And on this farm he had some ducks, E-I-E-I-O!
With a quack quack here and a quack quack there,
Here a quack there a quack everywhere a quack quack,
Old Macdonald had a farm, E-I-E-I-O.

Old Macdonald had a farm, E-I-E-I-O,
And on this farm he had some turkeys, E-I-E-I-O!
With a gobble gobble here and a gobble gobble there,
Here a gobble there a gobble everywhere a gobble gobble,
Old Macdonald had a farm, E-I-E-I-O.

   etc., etc.,

2. SONG FROM A CHILDREN'S GAME

The farmer wants a wife
The farmer wants a wife
Hey do diddledy ho
The farmer wants a wife

The wife wants a child
The wife wants a child
Hey do diddledy ho
The wife wants a child

The child wants a dog
The child wants a dog
Hey do diddledy ho
The child wants a dog

We all pat the dog
We all pat the dog
Hey do diddledy ho
We all pat the dog

One man went to mow, went to mow a meadow,
One man and his dog, went to mow a meadow

Two men went to mow, went to mow a meadow,
Two men,
One man and his dog, went to mow a meadow.

Three men went to mow, went to mow a meadow,
Three men, Two men,
One man and his dog, went to mow a meadow.

Four men went to mow, went to mow a meadow,
Four men, Three men, Two men,
One man and his dog, went to mow a meadow.

Five men went to mow, went to mow a meadow,
Five men, Four men, Three men, Two men,
One man and his dog, went to mow a meadow.

Six men went to mow, went to mow a meadow,
Six men,
Five men, Four men, Three men, Two men,
One man and his dog, went to mow a meadow.

Seven men went to mow, went to mow a meadow,
Seven men, Six men,
Five men, Four men, Three men, Two men,
One man and his dog, went to mow a meadow.

Eight men went to mow, went to mow a meadow,
Eight men, Seven men, Six men,
Five men, Four men, Three men, Two men,
One man and his dog, went to mow a meadow.

Nine men went to mow, went to mow a meadow,
Nine men, Eight men, Seven men, Six men,
Five men, Four men, Three men, Two men,
One man and his dog, went to mow a meadow!

COMPUTER OUTPUT

4. ALTERNATIVE METHOD

One man went to mow,went to mow a meadow
One man and his dog,went to mow a meadow

Two men went to mow,went to mow a meadow
Two men
One man and his dog,went to mow a meadow

Three men went to mow,went to mow a meadow
Three men
Two men
One man and his dog,went to mow a meadow

Four men went to mow,went to mow a meadow
Four men
Three men
Two men
One man and his dog,went to mow a meadow

Five men went to mow,went to mow a meadow
Five men
Four men
Three men
Two men
One man and his dog,went to mow a meadow

Six men went to mow,went to mow a meadow
Six men
Five men
Four men
Three men
Two men
One man and his dog,went to mow a meadow

Seven men went to mow,went to mow a meadow
Seven men
Six men
Five men
Four men
Three men
Two men
One man and his dog,went to mow a meadow

Eight men went to mow,went to mow a meadow
Eight men
Seven men
Six men
Five men
Four men
Three men
Two men
One man and his dog,went to mow a meadow

Nine men went to mow,went to mow a meadow
Nine men
Eight men

etc.

64

9

FROM MACHINE CODE TO FORTRAN

The practice of arithmetic is based on the representation of a number by a sequence of digits, each digit taking one of the values 0, 1, . . . up to but not including a maximum known as its radix, and representing a unit equal to the interpretation of the radix of the preceding digit (reading from right to left in most cases). Occasionally, as in sterling, the digits have different radixes; more usually all the digits have the same radix which may then be called the 'scale of notation'. Various methods of mechanization of the radix are possible — e.g. a wheel on a shaft with n detents mechanizes a digit of radix n. Electronically, a gas-filled tube with a central cathode and ten anodes around it is known as a decatron, and embodied in a circuit such that only one anode can carry a current at any moment, it is a representation of a decimal digit. Most electronic devices, however, either change their state smoothly, in which case they are not digital, or are either on or off, in which case they represent binary digits. For this reason most computers operate in binary, but the reason for this is almost purely practical, not theoretical. (Binary does have slight advantages in numerical analysis when numbers have to be expressed approximately, and so rounded off; this also makes precise definition of semantics in terms of character manipulation very difficult.)

Fundamental to the understanding of computers is the idea of the interpretation of a sequence of digits. Consider the sequence *251265*. Arithmetically, this is *251,265* — i.e. two hundred and fiftyone thousand, two hundred and sixtyfive. But thought of as *25.12.65*, it becomes Christmas day 1965! In the form *2.5.1265*, it could mean 'apply operation No.2 to the contents of accumulator No.5 and store location No.1265', and operation No.2 might be 'add the contents of the specified store location into the specified accumulator'. The dots are implicit, that is to say, if the sequence *251265* is to be added to something it is interpreted as *251,265*, but if it is to be obeyed it is interpreted as *2.5.1265*; the difference lies not in the way the sequence is stored, but in the circumstances in which it is used. This principle does not depend on the use of any particular scale of notation, although immediate application of it is prevented if an integer is presented in an inappropriate scale.

To relieve the sheer burden on the human memory, one gets into the habit of writing *2.5.1265* as *ADD.5.1265* as long as one is writing on paper, and of making the substitution only at the moment of preparing the final version for insertion into the machine. This is the second step away from pure machine language in most cases, the first (unless one's machine already works in decimal) being the use of decimal in place of the actual radix of the machine.

9.1 Machine code

A brief example will serve to convey the flavour of coding in machine language. Let us suppose that we wish to start a vector (x_1, x_2, x_3) at the value $(0, 0, 0)$. Before we can begin we have to decide on the store locations for these three numbers. Suppose that for some reason we have decided on locations 207, 208, 209. It is also necessary to decide where the instructions are going to be stored; let this be locations 50 onwards. The available instruction set is something we have to learn for each machine, but we can choose a fairly typical set for an early machine. The coding in the following sequence uses a method which is independent of the number of components in the vector; when this is three we lose on the deal, but though it is unnecessarily long it is better as an illustration than a shorter version would be:

50:	PutN	1 0000	Put the number 0 in accumulator 1
51:	PutN	2 0003	Put the number 3 in accumulator 2
52:	Store	2 0061	Put the contents of acc. 2 in location 61
53:	JumpZ	2 0062	Jump to the instruction in location 62 if the contents of acc. 2 are zero
54:	Add	2 0060	Add contents of loc. 60 into acc. 2
55:	Store	2 0056	Put contents of acc. 2 in location 56
56:	JumpU	0 0056	See below for explanation
57:	PutC	2 0061	Put contents of loc 61 into acc.2
58:	SubN	2 0001	Subtract the number 1 from the contents of acc. 2
59:	JumpU	0 0052	Jump to the instruction in location 52
60:	Store	1 0206	See below
61:	JumpU	0 0061	See below
62:	?		First instruction of next sequence

This sequence of instructions starts by putting zero into accumulator No.1 for storing in the x-locations, and '3' into accumulator No.2 as the suffix of the last component — we shall zeroize the components in reverse order. We then tuck the latter safely away in store because we are going to alter it in the accumulator. In fact, after checking that we have not finished, we convert the suffix k into an instruction 'store contents of acc. 1 in x_k' by adding it to an instruction to 'store contents of acc. 1 in x_0' which we have thoughtfully provided in location 60, and we store this manufactured instruction ahead of ourselves in

66

location 56 so that we shall come to it and obey it. The original contents of location 56 are thus of no consequence, and conventionally we make them something which will be both harmless and useful in case because of some sort of mistake (e.g. 55: Store 2 0156) we fail to overwrite it — namely, 'jump unconditionally to yourself', an instruction which will continue to be obeyed without doing anything at all, but will at least tell us what we have failed to do. We then reduce the index by one and recycle, taking care to leave the loop before attempting to put zero into the nonexistent x_0.

9.2 Assembly code

It may later become apparent that our choices of locations were unsuitable. If the reader will attempt to rewrite this sequence assuming that it is to be stored in locations 74 onwards and that the vector is stored in locations 30, 31, 32, he will appreciate the immense scope which long programmes in machine code give for errors due to silly slips and oversights. Most of these are eliminated in the following version:

```
*       = 0050 ⎫  These are not instructions but 'directives'
x0      = 0206 ⎭  for * see below
PutN    1 0000
PutN    2 0003
Store   2 WS+1   WS means the location labelled as such
JumpZ   2 WS+2
Add     2 WS
Store   2 *+1    * is a special label meaning 'here'
JumpU   0 *
PutC    2 WS+1
SubN    2 0001
JumpU   0 * − 7
WS:  Store   1 x0
JumpU   0 *
          ?
```

Such a version is said to be in Symbolic Assembly Code, because so many addresses are represented symbolically and not literally. The characteristics of this level of language are

1. It is the language of a particular machine, and in general it is meaningless with reference to any other
2. Its lines are more or less in one to one correspondence with the contents of individual locations in the machine, but,
3. A few of its lines are additional to the machine code and supply cross-referencing information, such as labels of working space, where the programme is to be stored, and so on. These are known as 'directives'. And
4. Some of the more advanced forms of symbolic assembly

language permit a limited macro-generation facility (one line corresponding to several machine instructions).

5. Although not illustrated above, symbolic assembly languages always permit alternative formats, namely, instructions and numerical constants, and usually there are alternative forms for constants. E.g. in the above language there might be permitted

DecF   0.271828
Alpha   RESULT =
Octal   000370

and so on. Usually (as here) this is done by means of 'pseudo-functions', that is, apparent functions which are not in the machine code itself.

Before a machine can accept its own symbolic assembly code, it must be provided with an assembly programme which will (1) do all conversions from decimal, (2) recognize its own functions and supply numerical values, (3) keep count of where it is putting things and keep a record of the meaning of labels and other symbolic quantities, (4) perform the arithmetic to deal with symbolic addresses such as 'WS+2', '* – 7', and (5) recognize and act upon its directive functions and constant formats. It should also (6) include some error detecting facilities.

At an elementary level it is fair to say that if a machine code is such that some sequences of digits are meaningless then it is simply inefficient with no compensating advantages. (At higher levels of design one has to take into account possibilities such as pre-set but variable-meaning orders, or the current vogue (to be deprecated, in the author's opinion) for functions which are 'reserved' to 'privileged' programmes because bad design renders their indiscriminate use dangerous.) But symbolic assembly language is redundant, and therefore provides certain scope for error detection and/or correction. It is highly desirable that an assembly programme should exploit this potential, and most of them do, at least so far as error detection is concerned. It is relatively easy, for example, for this programme to report constants which overflow the registers they are to be put into, references to labels which are nowhere defined, and so on. And usually all accidental misspellings are reported as errors — as 'illegal functions' if they occur in the function part of the format.

Because of this error-detecting facility, there is a lot to be said for making an assembly code, and not the true machine code, the lowest form of input to a machine, but if this is done then the assembly programme must be kept as compact as possible both as regards the space it occupies and in the time it takes to do its work, and this means foregoing luxurious extensions of it.

In this case, too, care should be taken that the symbolic assembly language allows one to say everything that the machine can do.

Assembly code designers should resist the temptation to be policemen except for overwhelming reasons. A new trend in design here is to start with the assembly language and to make it cover a range of machines with different machine codes. It is then made to exclude any coding which could produce different results on different machines, forcing inefficient working if necessary to this end.

9.3 Grammar of machine codes

Before leaving machine codes for good, it should be pointed out that few machines have a unique format for all their instructions. The grammar of a machine code is usually finite (polynomial) but it is often of a form of which the following is a simple example:

S ::= aA| bB   a ::= 0| 1| 2| 3
A ::= dC   b ::= 4| 5| 6| 7| 8| 9
B ::= DD   d ::= a| b
C ::= ddd
D ::= dd

With this grammar, productions can lead to any of the one hundred thousand numbers 00000–99999, and to nothing else, but those numbers beginning with 0, 1, 2 or 3 are interpreted according to the format $x.x.xxx$, and the rest according to the format $x.xx.xx$; thus format selection must wait on the identification of the first digit.

Machines with variable length instructions are also known; this is commonly the case where the natural word-length is too short to be adequate for every purpose, but also reflects the fact that the amount of information which an instruction has to convey varies. The means for indicating that a given sequence is incomplete and requires extension may or may not be recursive. There is one machine whose grammar as seen by the ordinary programmer can be written

⟨instrucn⟩ ::= ⟨funcn word⟩|⟨instrucn⟩⟨parameter word⟩

the number of parameter words being determined by the function. Character-based machines may operate similarly or may operate in reverse Polish notation.

9.4 Early autocodes

One leaves symbolic assembly languages and enters on autocodes as soon as one (a) places on the compiler the responsibility for assigning storage locations, and (b) abandons the one-to-one correspondence between the functions of the machine and the functions permitted in the language in favour of something nearer to mathematical notation. But at this level the freedom with which mathematical notation may be used is usually firmly, if not narrowly constrained. Autocode is specifically the name of a language designed for use on the Mercury computer (and of a predecessor known as Manchester Autocode). Generically it is extended to a number of consciously similar languages for other machines, and as descriptive of a language level it includes at least the earliest forms of Fortran. The latter, the name derived from 'FORmula TRANslator', was originally an American development for the IBM machines. The most widely used form is probably Fortran II (Rabinowitz, 1962), and remarks here, unless qualified to the contrary, mostly apply to that version. Fortran IV profited from the development of Algol, and includes a number of the features which we shall describe under Algol.

In the Manchester Autocode (Brooker, 1956), the programmer was required to reduce an expression like

$$x = a + b \times c + d \times e \tag{1}$$

into

$$
\begin{aligned}
v1 &= b \times c \\
v2 &= d \times e \\
v1 &= a + v1 \\
x &= v1 + v2
\end{aligned}
\tag{2}
$$

but was saved all truck with actual addresses in the machine, or with matters like initial clearing of accumulators, etc, for which a knowledge of the particular machine code is necessary. Provision was also made for limited instructions of the type

$$v2 = f(v1)$$

e.g. with $f = squareroot$. In Mercury Autocode and in Fortran the reduction of (1) to (2) was also mechanized subject to certain restrictions which arise fundamentally from the fact that at the time that they were announced the programming techniques necessary to implement recursively defined expressions had not been developed. They also accepted restrictions arising out of the machines for which they were developed (see the quotation from Brooker and Morris below). The appearance of tools of this sort was such a relief from coding in machine languages (even using symbolic assembly techniques) that their limitations were hardly noticed until some time later. By this time large vested interests had grown up, in the shape of users who swapped programmes and parts of programmes. In consequence, both languages tended to grow by having such additional facilities grafted on to them as could be added without interfering unduly with the basic facilities *in their original forms*.

In the original Mercury Autocode, for example, the letters $i, j \ldots t$ were available as integer variables and the others as real variables, and this rigidity has never been removed. In Fortran there was greater freedom in that multi-letter words could be used as the names of variables, but the initial letter of any name played a similar role (I to N integer, however) in determining its type. In Fortran IV this convention may be over-ruled by Algol-like declarations, but in order to accept, as far as possible, programmes written in earlier versions, the convention still holds unless overruled. Rather interestingly this has led to a new concept of much wider application (or at any rate it was the first example of the concept). This is the provision of a background of conventions so wide that it provides a 'default interpretation' whenever any statement of a declarative nature is omitted. The great virtue of this is that it eases enormously the preliminary burden of learning necessary to the casual user of the language before he can write a useful programme.

Consider also the matter of subscripting. In Mercury Autocode the syntax of variables is built up thus: we first define the following representative symbols

$$\langle \text{a-letter} \rangle ::= a|b|c|d|e|f|g|h|u|v|w|x|y|z$$
$$\langle \text{i-letter} \rangle ::= i|j|k|l|m|n|o|p|q|r|s|t$$
$$\langle \pi\text{-letter} \rangle ::= \langle \text{a-letter} \rangle | \pi$$
$$\langle \text{sign} \rangle ::= +|-$$

and the permitted structures for variables can now be shown as

$\langle \text{integer variable} \rangle ::= \langle \text{i-letter} \rangle$
  $\langle \text{real variable} \rangle ::= \langle \text{simple variable} \rangle | \langle \text{subscripted var} \rangle$
$\langle \text{simple variable} \rangle ::= \langle \text{a-letter} \rangle | \langle \text{a-letter} \rangle '$
$\langle \text{subscripted var} \rangle ::= \langle \pi\text{-letter} \rangle \langle \text{subscript} \rangle$
  $\langle \text{subscript} \rangle ::= \langle \text{integral numbers} \rangle | \langle \text{i-letter} \rangle | (\langle \text{i-letter} \rangle \langle \text{sign} \rangle$
      $\langle \text{integral number} \rangle)$

Thus $3, i, (j+2), (k-3)$ are all permitted as subscripts, but not $(i+j)$; the latter must be precomputed by, say, $m = i+j$. Also, whereas ab is a multiplied by b, ai is interpreted as a_i (one must write ia to get the product). In Fortran, because of multiletter names, the multiplication sign must be explicit (and because of the punched card influence it is an asterisk), and subscripts are bracketed. The curious distinction in Autocode between a-letters and π-letters 'is connected' according to Brooker and Morris (1962) 'with the layout of material in the high speed store of Mercury. For the present purpose we just have to accept it as an instance of the many awkward features that are likely to occur in practical autocodes'. It would be better now to say that this was the sort of thing that was always happening, in every language, in the late 1950's, but cannot be tolerated today.

It will also be seen that subscripts are single; that is, the array $a(1,1)$ . . . $a(3,3)$ must be treated as the vector $a(1)$ . . . $a(9)$,and $a(r,s)$ referenced by precomputing $m = 3(r-1)+s$. In Fortran II, in contrast, one, two or three subscripts were allowed, and up to seven in IBM Fortran IV. Subscripts to subscripts were still in the future.

9.5 Autocode and Fortran compared

Both Autocode and Fortran provided conditional jumps but not conditional expressions. The format was rather different. In Autocode the simple 'JUMP $\langle \text{label} \rangle$' was extended to

JUMP $\langle \text{label} \rangle$, $\langle \text{arith exp} \rangle \langle \text{relational op} \rangle \langle \text{arith exp} \rangle$

71

F

and in Fortran the unconditional 'GO TO ⟨label⟩' was replaced by

IF(⟨arith exp⟩), ⟨label⟩, ⟨label⟩, ⟨label⟩

all three labels being mandatory and being selected according as the arithmetic expression was less than, equal to or greater than zero. Fortran IV incorporates instructions of the 'IF (⟨boolean⟩)⟨statement⟩' type. Both languages, incidentally, use integer labels.

Again, both languages provided for a compact syntax for the writing of loops. In Autocode the simple assignment of a value to an i-letter could be expanded to the form

⟨i-letter⟩ = ⟨int.value⟩(⟨int.value⟩)⟨int.value⟩

and complemented by a statement 'REPEAT' lower down. The i-letter was then assigned the first of the integral values and the programme executed as far as the REPEAT; the programme then repeated this block of instructions as often as necessary with the i-letter increased each time by the second value until it executed it with the i-letter equal to the last value, when it ignored the REPEAT and continued. In Fortran the corresponding statement was

DO ⟨label⟩⟨int.var⟩ = ⟨int.exp⟩,⟨int.exp⟩,⟨int.exp⟩

with the increment in the *third* place on the right, and the label identifying the last instruction before the return point, which could be a dummy 'CONTINUE' whenever it was inconvenient to label an executive statement for the purpose. The i-letter in such a syntactical construct is known as the *controlled variable*. The precise syntax adopted is relatively uninteresting, but the semantics holds the possibility of all sorts of traps. What happens if the controlled variable is altered within the block that is being repeated — is the change accepted at the next incrementation, or nullified, or is such a manoeuvre illegal? How is the final test made? In Autocode the second variable could be positive or negative, but the final test was on equality, and a loop such as $i = 1(2)6$ would loop for ever with $i = 1, 3, 5, 7 \ldots$ In Fortran the test was a 'greater than', avoiding this trap, but all three values had to be positive. What is the value of the controlled variable on exit — the last accepted value or the first rejected one? The answers to these questions can take much space and are only of historical interest now; what is significant is that their importance has now been recognized, and the answers are a part of the specification of any language proposed today, and not, as in those days, the result of the way the first compiler was written.

Both languages made provision for the natural handling of subroutines and functions, the parameters being evaluated down to the state of a machine address if possible, or to a single value in the case of an expression, before entry to the routine; this is effectively what has since been described as call by simple name.

Whenever subscripted variables are involved, it is necessary to give the machine some indication of the amount of storage required by specifying the number of components to which each subscripted variable can run. In Autocode this was done by directives of the form $a \to 20$, implying that in addition to the simple variables a and a', storage for a vector a with suffixes running from 0 to 20 is needed. A series of such directives caused consecutive allocation of storage, so that if this was followed by $c \to 5$, then a call for a_{22} would yield c_1. This would normally be the result of erroneous programming but was occasionally exploited. The corresponding facility in Fortran was the 'DIMENSION statement', and one such as

$$\text{DIMENSION A}(2,3)$$

provided the information that A was the name, *not of a simple variable* (contrast this with Autocode) *nor of a function but of an array* whose suffixes run from *1(sic)* to 2 and from *1* to *3*. Going out of bounds was monitored in the course of finding a required address.

Finally, because the high-speed store of Mercury was small, an Autocode programme had to be written in terms of a number of 'chapters' each limited in size to what the high speed store would hold. (In case of chapter overflow the monitor referred the programme back to its writer for revision.) Each chapter had its own labels, and special arrangements were provided for going 'across' or 'down' into other chapters ('down' implying a return 'up' later). Chapter 0 was always the last in a programme and was the signal for entry into the execution phase. A Fortran programme was organized in terms of named subroutines and an unnamed main routine; 'CALL ⟨subroutine⟩' arranged the transfer into a subroutine and 'RETURN' the exit back to the calling routine. It was always a claim of Fortran devotees that while compilation might sometimes be slow, no routine need be compiled more than once, since a complete programme could be assembled with some parts in Fortran and some already compiled into machine code. Provision was made for a declaration 'COMMON' to indicate that the variables so declared were not local to the routine but global. To this concept was added another declaration 'EQUIVA-LENCE' which permitted the same storage area to be called by different names within a routine. Unfortunately different interpretations of the interaction between these two declarations have resulted in an incompatibility between Fortran II and Fortran IV, so that programmes in the former can not always be compiled as though in a subset of the latter.

As a result of this difficulty and of a growing number of local variations, a committee was set up in 1962, and in 1964 a draft standard specification was published (Heising, 1965) for two languages to be known as Fortran and Basic Fortran. These are as compatible as possible with the various existing versions of Fortran IV and Fortran II respectively, and Basic Fortran is defined as a strict subset of Fortran. The Fortran specification is a document of some

16,000 words and that for Basic Fortran is a duplicate with some omissions and some consequent modifications. (The number of words in this book is about 60,000.)

9.6 Jovial

In 1958 the committee who were working on Algol produced an interim report which proved, in retrospect, to have two main results. By introducing CBNF to the world it inspired the earliest work on syntax directed compilers. And it inspired a team under Jules Schwartz at System Development Corporation to improve on its linguistic proposals and develop Jovial (Shaw, 1963). This language resembles the music of Bach, which one critic has described as 'a hundred years behind its times and a hundred years in advance of every other time'; which is regarded with suspicion by the world at large and with devotion by everyone who has taken the trouble to understand it. Lacking some features which appeared in Algol 60, it contains others which are still being hailed as new when some new language or system introduces them (e.g. the ability to modify itself to suit an individual programmer's notational preferences). It contains features which make it well suited for programming (a) *very* large systems, in which (b) a number of programmes operate independently on a common data pool, and (c) operator communication in English is desirable; its largest area of application has been the writing of programmes for the American Air Defence System.

IO

COBOL

The main drive for the development of Cobol (a COmmon Business Oriented Language) came from the United States Department of Defense. It is very difficult to have a truly objective opinion about it, since in some directions it has set its sights extraordinarily high and in others its attitude is almost cringing. Its distinguishing features, which is shares with a number of industrially sponsored languages such as the Honeywell 'Fact', the N.C.R. Language H, and the I.C.T. 'Nebula' are:

1. It attempts to be a subset of English, and as such readable (though not writeable) by the uninitiated,
2. It caters for data structures of the sort found in typical office records, whether personnel, stores, financial, or a combination of these,
3. It aims at a realistic approach to the attainment of complete compatibility.

As regards the first of these, we discuss subsets of English later, and it will suffice here to recall (with approval) one sarcastic comment about the assumption that there are people for whom it is necessary to make allowances, who can understand the meaning *and implications of*

MOVE X TO Y.

ADD BALANCE TO OLDTOTAL GIVING NEWTOTAL

but are unable to do the same for

$Y = X$; $NEWTOTAL = OLDTOTAL + BALANCE$

The strength of Cobol lies in (2) and (3) above. A Cobol programme is punched to a quite rigid format and a lot can turn on whether eight or nine blanks occur before the first visible character in a line. Its designers did not envisage load-and-go operation. The compiler produces two things, a programme in machine language punched in a form suitable for feeding into a machine for immediate obedience, and a printed copy of the original Cobol edited in certain respects (i.e. a documentation to accompany the punched output). In the simplest case the editing may be no more than the insertion of the date of compilation for reference. At the other extreme, an I.C.T.

Rapidwrite compiler produces a text in true Cobol although the input is in a subset of Cobol so simplified by various conventional abbreviations that purists refuse to allow it to be called a form of Cobol at all.

The original Cobol report appeared in April 1960, and a revised specification appeared in June 1961. This consists of 'required' and 'elective' elements. Strictly speaking this distinction is not part of the language but of the examination syllabus in the language. A compiler 'passes' if it translates correctly all required elements, and passes 'with honours' if it correctly translates the elective features as well. In November 1963, E.C.M.A., the European Computer Manufacturer's Association, produced proposals for 'Compact Cobol', in which the boundary between 'required' and 'elective' is shifted in the direction of requiring less, with the object of assisting small machines. The maintenance of Cobol is in the hands of a committee appointed by CODASYL (Conference on Data Systems Languages), or was — at the time of writing there are rumours of a change here.

10.1 Programme structure

A Cobol programme is in four parts known as divisions. These are the Identification, Environment, Data and Procedure divisions.The last of these contains the programme proper, but this is meaningless (or at best incomplete) without the pre-supposition of a data structure to work upon defined in the third division. The environment and data divisions are further divided into sections, the former into configuration and input-output sections and the latter into file, working-storage and constant sections. A division or section is headed by its name, followed by a full stop, on a line to itself. The contents of a section or division consists of sentences grouped into named paragraphs.

The identification division is small and relatively fixed in format. For example

```
000100  IDENTIFICATION DIVISION.
000200  PROGRAM-ID.    PAYROLL.
000400  AUTHOR.    JOHN DOE.
000450  DATE-WRITTEN.    APRIL 5TH
000460      1960.
000500  SECURITY.
000600  INSTALLATION.
000700  DATE-COMPILED. TODAY.
000800  REMARKS.
```

The card numbering system has been explained in Section 6.1. Any or all of the paragraphs after the second may be omitted; their names are fixed. The programme name must be a proper Cobol word, in effect a sequence of not more than 30 characters constructed from the numerals, the letters and the hyphen (used internally). This division is copied on to the listed output, replacement of the contents of DATE-COMPILED by the actual date being an elective feature; nothing else is done with it.

10.2 The environment division

The Environment division is supposed to contain all that information which is needed to solve compatibility problems, although not necessarily explicitly. This consists of a description of the computer on which the translation is to be done, a similar description of the computer on which the compiled programme is intended to be run (not necessarily the same machine), an indication of any cross-referencing of names which may be necessary when referring to peripherals and so on.

In practice, the valuable information which can be conveyed in this division lies at a lower level than its wording might suggest. A Cobol compiler is a big enough programme in any case, without trying to give it a multi-lingual output, in terms of the machine order-codes it can use. And one might also very reasonably suppose that the only purpose the SOURCE-COMPUTER paragraph could possibly serve would be a similar one to the DATE-COMPILED paragraph — viz., that on the listed output the computer actually used would sign its own name. But commercial computers are sold in varying 'configurations'; that is, a machine may be advertised as fitted with a minimum of two, maximum of eight, tape units, and your installation may have six. So although it is quite possible, by compiling first into an intermediate language (probably of some sort of macrogenerator type) to write a compiler with a multilingual output, it is of greater practical advantage to write a compiler which can automatically adapt the efficiency of the object programme to the configuration of the machine on which it is to be run. And this applies even to the name of the source computer, since although the compiler must be written for the machine on which it is to be run, it can be made self-adapting to the configuration, again with possible implications on the efficiency of the object programme, and even adapt itself in emergency to a configuration which has been temporarily reduced by a peripheral breakdown.

A typical example of the Environment Division might begin thus:

```
001101   ENVIRONMENT DIVISION.
001201   CONFIGURATION SECTION.
001302   SOURCE-COMPUTER. COPY ME.
001402   OBJECT-COMPUTER. BIG-BROTHER
001412   6 TAPE-UNITS.
001503   SPECIAL-NAME. TYPEWRITER IS TELEPRINTER.
001601   INPUT-OUTPUT SECTION.
```

and continue with I-O section material. In this example we have used the final digit of the card sequence number for reference purposes. Thus those that end in '1' are absolutely fixed in format, apart from the general rule which allows the separator between the words to consist of any number of spaces. In the computer names, reference 2, two formats are allowed, of which both are shown. COPY can be followed by any Cobol name which has been used to identify a suitable description which is kept stored in a part of the computer memory called the Cobol library. Alternatively a detailed description (in general more complicated than the example) can be given, and the manner in which this should be done is not laid down in Cobol itself, but is left to the compiler writer to lay down. In this way the writer of a compiler for a bizarre installation — e.g. one containing a microphone/loudspeaker for in/output — would not be impossibly constrained by rules which had not foreseen it. The paragraph SPECIAL-NAME, reference 3, is more straightforward; it means that (1) the procedure division, possibly originally written with some other installation in mind, refers to a teleprinter, (2) there is on the object computer a peripheral which the compiler writer always calls the typewriter, and (3) this is what is to be used when the procedure division asks for the teleprinter. The name of this paragraph is permitted to be in the plural, and the paragraph to contain as many such sentences as are required (the rest of the paragraph being indented four spaces, like the '1960' in the identification division).

The INPUT-OUTPUT SECTION is concerned with similar correspondences of names between data-files and the hardware items on which they are to be read or written — these are in a paragraph with the fixed name FILE-CONTROL — and also optionally with certain RERUN facilities — these are in a paragraph with the fixed name I-O-CONTROL.

10.3 Further details
The grammar of Cobol is not written in CBNF but in a less general notation peculiar to it and a few languages which resemble it fairly closely. The sentences in a FILE-CONTROL paragraph will serve to illustrate it; they must conform to the following format:

SELECT [*OPTIONAL*] file-name-1 [*RENAMING* file-name-2]

ASSIGN TO [integer-1] hardware-name-1 [, hardware-name-2]

[FOR *MULTIPLE REEL*] [, *RESERVE* $\begin{Bmatrix} \text{integer-2} \\ \text{NO} \end{Bmatrix}$

ALTERNATE $\begin{Bmatrix} \text{AREAS} \\ \text{AREA} \end{Bmatrix}$] [*SELECT*...] .

In this schema, words in lower case are type names such as would be in metalinguistic brackets in CBNF, but the '-1' and '-2' are explicit signs of what is tacit in CBNF, namely, that the replacements are independent. (Cf. Section 7.4.) Words in capitals appear literally; those not *italicised* are 'noise words', allowed but unnecessary and contributing nothing. No other noise words are permitted. Braces show alternatives, and square brackets mean that their contents may be omitted or included according to the meaning required. The simplest FILE-CONTROL paragraph would therefore be something like:

```
001704  FILE-CONTROL. SELECT CONTROL-SEQUENCE
001800    ASSIGN PAPER-READER.
```

but in addition to the possibility of a whole series of SELECTs, any individual one can expand thus

```
001704  FILE-CONTROL. SELECT OPTIONAL SUPPLEMEN
001800 - TARIES RENAMING MASTER ASSIGN TO 1
001900    TAPE-UNIT FOR MULTIPLE REEL, RESERVE
002000    1 ALTERNATE AREA
```

Here CONTROL-SEQUENCE, SUPPLEMENTARIES and MASTER are the names of files; PAPER-READER is the name used in this installation for a paper tape reader. OPTIONAL means that the programme is not to mind if this file is absent during a run which does not take a course that requires it. FOR MULTIPLE REEL is concerned with files that take more than one reel and therefore require action of an unusual sort when the file is half read, and RE-NAMING is rather a misnomer (STRUCTURED ON would be better) since it means that file-name-1 has not been described in the Data division because it is exactly like file-name-2. ALTERNATE, of course, does not mean 'alternate', but 'alternative'.

RESERVE raises a point which deserves a slightly longer look. Computers cannot look at information on magnetic tape just as and when they like, so they have to take a copy of a part of it and refer to their copy, which is usually known as a buffer. Since a programme which has finished with what is in its buffer will be held up until the next bit of tape has been copied, it may pay off in speed to be extravagant in storage demands by using two (or more) buffer areas, used alternately (or cyclically), so that one is being copied into while another is being worked upon. This is the function of the RESERVE clause. The reason we note it specially here is that it is concerned with communication of an unusual type of information — effectively a policy preference in the manner of compilation — a type which most programming languages do not cater for at all.

We presume that only middle-sized machines take any notice of RESERVE; the small ones have to say, 'Sorry, but we just haven't the extra space available', and the large ones say, 'Look, chum, if it's any use to you on this time-sharing system by which you don't pay if you are forced to wait, we give it to you without your asking for it'. This is rather like air-mail stickers which are a waste of time (a) on journeys too short for air, but also (b) for destinations to which the post office uses the currently quickest route irrespective. Be this as it may, we do call attention to the fact that Cobol finds it desirable to communicate not only instructions as to how the data reduction is to be carried out, but also advice as to the preferred method of organizing data queues.

To summarize, any nasty taste (and there usually is one) which a study of the Environment division leaves on people more familiar with other languages should not be blamed on Cobol as a language, but on the nastiness of the compatibility situation which it tries to face more honestly and completely than more mathematical languages have to do, or than industrially sponsored languages (which often have a minor aim of selling a particular group of machines) always wish to do.

10.4 The Data division

The DATA DIVISION is based on the concept of a FILE and consists of a series of file-descriptions together with a small amount of material (working space and constants) which does not fit into a file-structure. A file consists of an indefinite number of RECORDS all of which conform to one or other of a small number of structure patterns contained in the Data division, and it is presumed that when a file is READ, it is the next record that is read, and that when the name of a file is used in the Procedure division it is the last-read record from that file that is meant. Thus unless provision is made to preserve data in working space, successive records are dealt with independently. The implication is that each file referred to by an ASSIGN in the Environment division will be given a buffer area adequate to hold one record of the (maximum) size shown by its description in the Data division to be necessary. However, although this is the basic theory, a record may be an inconveniently small unit for the mechanism of the magnetic tape, and the concept of a BLOCK of records is introduced to get around this. In its physical form as a magnetic tape, a file may well begin with a title or LABEL; such material can be of two sorts, the first in a form laid down by the person in charge of the installation, to ensure that tapes do not get mixed up or otherwise wrongly used, and the second in a form desired by the programmer. Concerning the former nothing can be said and it is laid down that the latter must be regarded as an alternative form of record. Provision is therefore made to describe LABELS simply as STANDARD or OMITTED. (Oddly, in view of the wish to attain as high a degree of compatibility as possible, the alternative FOREIGN is not provided, though if it were, it would be necessary to have a universally accepted standard method for recognizing the *end* of the label.)

The remaining part of the description of a file consists of a description of the records it may contain. This is best detailed by an example. The 'F' of 'FD' stands in Col. 8, and the three hyphens in Col. 7.

```
FD  COSTS-FILE; BLOCK CONTAINS 10 RECORDS; LABEL
    RECORDS ARE STANDARD; VALUE OF IDENTIFICA
-   TION IS 'COSTS'; DATA RECORDS ARE WAGE-ITEM,
    PURCHASE-ITEM, DEPENDING ON ITEM.
01  WAGE-ITEM.
    02  ITEM; SIZE IS 1 AN.
    88  WAGE-TYPE; VALUE IS 'W'.
    02  EMPLOYEE-DATA.
        03  EMPLOYEE-NO; SIZE IS 6 NUMERIC DISPLAY.
        03  SALARY; SIZE IS 4 COMPUTATIONAL
        03  BONUS-CODE; SIZE IS 3 AN.
    02  ITEM-DATA.
        03  PROJECT-NO; PICTURE IS 999999X.
        03  NORMAL-TIME; SIZE IS 3 COMPUTATION
-           AL; POINT LEFT 1.
        03  OVERTIME; SIZE IS 3 COMPUTATIONAL;
            POINT LEFT 1.
01  PURCHASE-ITEM.
    02  ITEM; SIZE IS 1 AN.
    88  PURCHASE-TYPE; VALUE IS 'P'.
    02  INVOICE-NO; PICTURE IS AAX99999.
    02  DEBIT-VALUE; SIZE IS 8; USAGE IS COMPUTA
-       TIONAL; POINT LOCATION IS LEFT 3 PLACES.
    02  PROJECT-NO; PICTURE IS 999999X.
```

So far as the FD portion is concerned, note, in addition to what has already been said, that 'VALUE OF . . . ' means that the standard label of the correct file will include the word 'COSTS' as a check that the file is the right one, and that 'DEPENDING ON . . . ' is a Honeywell idiom meaning that, the records being of two types, the type to which a given record belongs can be determined immediately by inspection of the field 'ITEM'. Thus the two '01' portions are alternative possibilities. Two records from this file might read

W1428571950NIL004321 217000   PJJ-0021400063550004321

which we interpret initially by dividing them thus

W/142857/1950/NIL/004321 /217/000/
P/JJ-00214/00063550/004321 /

in accordance with the data descriptions. In both types, that is, the first 'element' is a single alphanumeric character (1 AN). If this is 'W', it is followed by (i) the employee number, consisting of six numerical characters, (ii) his salary, a four decimal-digit number already in the most convenient form for computation (probably binary), (iii) a bonus-code symbol of three alphanumeric characters, (iv) the project number, of six decimal digits and a general character (in this office either space or asterisk and in this example a space), (v) the normal time, which in this example was *21.7 hrs*, and so on.

The indentations, after the first, are optional; it is the level-numbers which define the tree-structure. The term 'data-item' is used to cover 'elements', complete 'records', and also intermediate items such as EMPLOYEE-DATA. Thus because this term is used in the syntactical description of MOVE, it is possible to say

MOVE EMPLOYEE-DATA IN COSTS-FILE TO EMPLOYEE-DATA IN REPORT-FILE

(this is a copying process, but the word COPY is reserved for copying *from the library*). Levels may go up to the generous limit of 49, with 66, 77, 88 serving special purposes. 88 introduces a 'condition name' and as used in our example it enables one to write

READ COSTS-FILE. IF WAGE-TYPE THEN . . .

(instead of IF ITEM EQUAL TO 'W' . . .) . When a structure shows a repetitive pattern, it may be described once with 'OCCURS integer-1 TIMES', and the item so described must then be subscripted when used in the Procedure division. If a part of a record is irrelevant to the programme, it may be referred to by the name FILLER in the Data division.

Files belong essentially to the external world and must be brought in and out, one record at a time, by READ and WRITE. In addition to the FILE SECTION there are similarly organized WORKING-STORAGE and CONSTANT SECTIONs, with level 77 available for items that do not fit into a structure. These sections are for material which never gets outside the machine. VALUE may be used to initialize such material. In Compact Cobol the CONSTANT section is merged into the WORKING-STORAGE section and 01 is used instead of 77.

10.5 The procedure division

Concerning the PROCEDURE DIVISION, a colleague once remarked to me that 'Cobol ceases to be interesting once you understand it', and there is some truth in this. If we allow that IF means EVALUATE THE BOOLEAN AND THEN . . . , then every statement begins with an imperative verb, and the grammar is simply a list of the structures permitted after each verb — all different, since even ADD. . . TO and MULTIPLY . . . BY have different prepositions. The problem in Cobol has been the semantics, in many fields, but particularly where editing is required. And there has been the sorry story (not unknown in other languages, but aggravated by

82

pressure from the Department of Defense) of competing implementers producing different interpretations of intricate cases, often
with the result that the intricate case has been declared illegal in the
language. For example, it is possible to write, for a sum of less than
£100 to the nearest 2/–, PICTURE IS 99V9, PICTURE IS 99·9 or
USAGE IS COMPUTATIONAL POINT 1 LEFT. £6.10s would
then be stored as the characters 065, the characters 06.5, or the number 65 in binary, respectively. In MOVing this value, the editing required is obvious, and will be done. But arithmetic is banned on the
second, though not between items in the first and third styles. It has
also been necessary to say that 'it is illegal to MOVE a group item
whose format is such that editing would be required on the elements
in separate operations'. All this is the result of a struggle between the
linguistic requirements and the state of the art several years ago, in
which the latter won, thereby stamping Cobol as a language of the
early sixties.

In one respect, Cobol appears to be a non-pure-procedural
language. Given a paragraph which consists of a single statement
'GO TO . . . ' , one can write elsewhere 'ALTER paragraph TO
PROCEED TO . . . ' . This oddity is more apparent than real, as it is
no more than a means of expressing a switch, or (an initialized)
variable of type label. Cobol also has the switch, since it can say
'GO TO label-1, label-2 . . . DEPENDING ON integer-variable'.

In most languages a subroutine is either open or closed. That is, if
it is required more than once it is either repeated at both places (open)
or it is completely detached, given a name, and called by this name
at both places. Cobol does not make this distinction. Sentences are
grouped into paragraphs with names, and paragraphs may be further
grouped into sections if desired. The verb PERFORM, followed by
any paragraph or section name, calls in that paragraph or section as a
subroutine, but if the same paragraph is entered in sequence it is left
in sequence. The standard form of the exit is the sequential one; it is
modified by the PERFORM before the entry, and resets itself after
use. (This description defines what happens when it is jumped to in
the middle.) This verb is a complicated one; in Compact Cobol its
only other syntax is the addition of 'THRU paragraph-name-2',
which causes the execution of paragraph-name-1 to paragraph-name-
2 (inclusive), but standard Cobol uses it also to provide compact
coding of loops by providing for '*n* times', 'until. . . ' , and 'varying
. . . by . . . ' with nesting of up to three controlled variables. Cobol
does not provide for subroutines with parameters in the usual sense;
a library subroutine can be introduced by 'COPY routine-name
[USING variable-name-1 . . .] ' but if it is required with different
parameters in different places then distinct copies are created.

In addition to the usual 'IF . . . ' , Cobol has another form of conditional dictated by the file concept but adapted also to deal with the

83

trap on numerical overflow. The syntax of a READ statement is

READ file-name RECORD [*INTO* data-name] [AT *END* imperative statement]

and the third portion of this is equivalent to 'if the result is not another record but an end-of-file indicator then . . . ' . A similar phrase 'ON SIZE ERROR . . . ' deals with overflow in arithmetic processes.

One problem which has to be faced by all languages modelled on a natural language is whether and to what extent words can be reserved. The Compact Cobol report lists 226 words which are part of the Cobol system and should be avoided — and does not include SORT among them, although a 'sorting' verb has been the subject of much study (Paterson [1963]). There is no reason why use of the word OMITTED as the name of a file should ever cause ambiguity, but one is told that it is unsafe to try to do so. The real problem in a situation like this is that, if words are reserved wholesale (i.e. not just the inevitables, whatever they may be) then all the words of the *extended* language must be reserved to the *minimum* one.

The above description and comment has concentrated on those features of Cobol which distinguish it from other languages, and in particular those arising from problems which languages in other classes do not have to meet. In other respects it is of its time — e.g. it allows for subscripting, but not being recursive, up to three subscripts only, and no subscripts to subscripts. Nested calls of subroutines are possible subject to elaborate rules which, among other things, rule out all recursive calls. Subroutines cannot raise their own storage and the division between data and procedure divisions is absolute. Working storage must be anticipated by providing it in the Data division under level 77. The Environment division is something new. It is therefore interesting to see that in Algol subscripting is completely free, subroutines can be freely called without checking whether the context permits it, they may be called with parameters and may raise their own storage. But there is no environment division in Algol 60, and only a rudimentary one when the in/output proposals are added, though there are proposals within the maintenance organization for a radically new approach to environment problems (See Section 15.2.1). The reserved word problem has been shelved for as long as we wish by printing reserved words, used in their technical capacity, in black type.

84

11

ALGOL

The appearance of the 'Report on the Algorithmic Language ALGOL 60' (Naur, 1960) marked a very great step forward in the subject of programming languages. (For the preliminary report of 1958 see Section 9.6. The so-called 'Algol 58' was the subject of some experiments in compiler writing but as a working language was never much more than a rallying cry for reactionaries.) The major characteristics of Algol, which should be taken into account when describing any language as Algol-like, are

(a) Use of CBNF to define syntax, with semantics in English,
(b) Acceptance of as much of current mathematical notation as could be proved workable, with elimination of all arbitrary restrictions whose origin lay in compiler design.
(c) A clear distinction in symbolism between the imperative (assignment) equals and the predicative (relational) equals
(d) Use of black-type English words (or underlining) to supply such new symbols as it required
(e) Page lay-out completely at the service of legibility to human readers. (Not even a single space has any semantic significance, which may have been going too far.)

The deficiencies of Algol, which we discuss in Section 11.4, would appear all to be due to its authors' awareness that they were making a big step forward and their determination not to overstep their abilities in the circumstances (which included the usual need to work to some sort of target date). In fact, a few slips were made, the more obvious of which were cleared up in a revised report in 1962. Maintenance of Algol is now in the hands of IFIP (the International Federation for Information Processing) and an Algol Bulletin (published from the Mathematical Centre at Amsterdam) serves as a forum for exploring its maintenance problems.

In the syntax, integral and real numbers are first built up from the numerals, the plus and minus signs, the decimal point and the symbol $_{10}$. (Thus $3 \cdot 5_{10} + 6$ means $3 \cdot 5 \times 10^{+6}$.) Names, referred to as 'identifiers', are built up by

$\langle \text{identifier} \rangle ::= \langle \text{letter} \rangle | \langle \text{identifier} \rangle \langle \text{letter} \rangle | \langle \text{identifier} \rangle \langle \text{numeral} \rangle$

that is, as any sequence of letters or numerals beginning with a letter. No identifier may be used without a 'declaration' of the type of object it names, except for labels, whose very use defines them. ⟨Simple arithmetic expression⟩s are built up as in Language 3 of Section 7.2.This corresponds to normal practice except that it would leave a/bc meaning $(a/b)c$ etc. But this particular case does not arise in quite this blatant form, because, owing to the use of multi-letter identifiers, the multiplication sign must never be suppressed. Special notation for exponentiation and suffixing enable the input string to be kept strictly linear; x^y becomes $x \uparrow y$, where y may be a name (simple or suffixed identifier), an unsigned number, or any expression in brackets, and $x_{y,z}$ becomes $x[y,z]$, where y and z may themselves be expressions which may be or contain subscripted variables. The notation $f(x)$ for the function f of x is available, and is used for all more complicated purposes: thus

$$\sum_{x=m}^{n} p_x \quad \text{becomes} \quad \text{sigma(p[x],x,m,n).}$$

But subject to these notational hurdles, if an expression is meaningful and valid in algebra, however involved it may be, it is valid in Algol with the same meaning. A similar development from the values **true** and **false**, the relational operators between numbers ('$=$', '$>$', etc), and the boolean operators embeds boolean algebra into the language in the same way. Conditional expressions are built up by the productions

⟨simple expression⟩ ::= ... |(⟨cond.exp⟩)
⟨cond.exp⟩ ::= **if** ⟨boolean exp⟩ **then** ⟨simple expression⟩ **else** ⟨expression⟩

The range of structures which this grammar permitted was not in itself enough to force compiler writers to abandon non-recursive techniques, but was a strong pointer in this direction.

Algol is a procedural language, programmes being built up from units (called 'statements') each containing its own imperative(s). The elementary unit takes one of three forms:

(1) X := Y (2) **go to** Z (3) a name

where X is a simple name or a subscripted name, Y an expression, and Z a label-name or a designational expression (a conditional label-name or a switch (see below) or combination of these). In the third form the name is a procedure name (see next Section). Such elementary units are separated by semicolons, as are the compound units formed by surrounding a sequence of units by **begin** . . . **end**. Statements as well as expressions may be conditional, and the inclusion of the option by which

if B **then** Z; is equivalent to **if** B **then** Z **else**;

(i.e. to 'Z if B, dummy if not B') while a very natural mode of expression, has been a fruitful source of unexpected ambiguities.

A programme is a single self-contained statement, that is to say it is a message in the form **begin** . . . **end** which uses no names whose meaning it does not define (or which are not system defined). Declarations must be made immediately after a **begin** and are valid up to the *corresponding* **end**; this makes them effectively imperatives for the creation of the objects they refer to before value-assigning imperatives are reached, and allows such creation to be temporary if there is any point in arranging it this way. The permitted types are 'real', 'integer', 'boolean' and arrays of these; thus '**begin real** x, y; . . .' means 'start this phase by assigning further storage for two real numbers to be called x and y; throughout this phase x and y refer to these numbers whatever may be the case elsewhere'. However, the further types 'string', 'label' and 'procedure' are permitted to *bound* variables, as we shall see, and an object of type 'switch' permits indirect reference to labels; this is an array of labels or expressions of type label that is embedded in the message and not in created storage.

11.1 The development of the procedure

Although the fully recursive nature of the syntax of expressions may have suggested recursive methods in implementation, it is in fact possible to implement by non-recursive methods any programme in which the degree of nesting can be determined explicitly by a preliminary scan. However Algol permits routines to be written in which the depth of recursion cannot be determined until run time. Mostly this is due to the development, out of the subroutine, of the procedure. The following account of how this happened may not be strictly historical but cannot be far off being so.

In the notation of algebra, we can express the fact that the H.C.F. of three numbers is that of any two with the third thus

$$\text{HCF}(a, b, c) = \text{hcf}(\text{hcf}(a, b), c)$$

In Algol, a sequence for reducing both of two numbers to their h.c.f. might be written

> A: **if** x = y **then go to** Z;
>   **if** x $\rangle$ y **then** x := x − y **else** y := y − x;
>   **go to** A;
> Z:

and (without bothering to improve on this) we consider the problem of using it to find the h.c.f. of three numbers, *a*, *b* and *c*, given on an input tape. We assume that the system specifies that the name *next* always refers to the next value in the input tape, and that *print* (*x*) similarly provides us with an output facility. At a level of programming which is very close to machine-practice language, we should have to see that x and y are started with the correct contents and that

87

proper return information ('link') is organized. A complete pro-gramme along these lines would be

```
begin integer a, b, c, n, x, y; comment see text;
       a := next;  b := next;  c := next;
       x := a;  y := b;  n := 1;  comment setting operands
          and link for first use of subroutine;
A:  if x = y then go to Z;
    if x ⟩ y then x := x – y else y := y – x;
    go to A;
Z:  if n = 1 then go to B else if n = 2 then go to C;
B:  y := c;  n := 2;  go to A;  comment second setting,
       but x already contains the appropriate value;
C:  print(x)  end.
```

This is over-elementary and can be simplified. (1) Only three of *a, b, c, x, y* are really necessary. (2) One can use a switch by replacing the first **comment** by 'switch S := B, C;' and line Z by '**go to** S[n];'. But the *link* planting is clumsy and could be eliminated if one could do something like

```
begin integer a, b, c, x, y;
       a := next;  b := next;  c := next;  x := a;  y := b;
H:  begin A: if x = y then go to Z;
                if x ⟩ y then x := x – y else y := y – x;
                go to A;  Z: end;
    y := c;  perform H;  print(x) end.
```

as indeed one can in Cobol, although the *parameter* planting is now looking clumsy. There is some evidence (the **do** of the 1958 report) that this direction of development was considered, but if so, then it was seen to be outclassed by the following alternative:

```
begin integer a, b, c, x, y;
       procedure H;  begin A: if x = y then go to Z;
                           if x ⟩ y then x := x – y else y := y – x;
                           go to A;  Z: end;
       a := next;  b := next;  c := next;
       x := a;  y := b;  H;
       y := c;  H;  print(x) end.
```

For now it becomes possible to deal with the parameters in a way that matches conventional mathematical practice. We write

```
begin integer a, b, c;
       procedure H(x,y); comment 1;
          begin A: if x = y then go to Z;
                      if x ⟩ y then x := x – y else y := y – x;
                      go to A;  Z: end;
       a := next;  b := next;  c := next;
       H(a, b);  H(a, c);  print(a) end.
```

At **comment** 1, it is permissible to assist the compiler by inserting '**integer** x, y;', thus indicating that x and y are intended to be replaced by other variables of type integer, and many compilers demand this assistance. Such information on bound variables is called 'specification' as opposed to the 'declaration' of free variables; it is not a storage-raising imperative in the sense in which a declaration is (but see Section 5.1 above, and **value** below). The statement $H(a, b)$ means 'carry on as though you had here a copy of the "body" of the definition of H with a and b taking the place of x and y respectively, each time they occur'. Thus $H(a,b)$ reduces both a and b to their h.c.f., and $H(a,c)$ reduces the reduced a and c to *their* h.c.f.

This last feature is something which does not arise in the static conditions of algebra. In many circumstances it is just what we want; in others it is most inconvenient. To avoid it, a variation is provided in which we would write the procedure declaration thus:

    procedure H(x,y,z);   **value** x,y;
      begin A: **if** x = y **then go to** Z;
          if x $\rangle$ y **then** x := x – y **else** y := y – x;
          go to A;   Z: z := x **end**;

The **value** specification requires the procedure to start by making local copies of the values of x and y and to do all further work on these copies. It now becomes necessary to find a way of getting the answer out of the procedure; this is the purpose of z which is not given a value specification. The main programme would read

      ... **integer** a, b, c, d; ...
      H(a,b,d);   H(d,c,d);   print(d) **end**

But in all this we are still one step short of the algebraic notation by which $hcf(a,b)$ is not 'how to get' the h.c.f., but is its actual value. A name cannot be both of these at once, and it has been made possible to define it either way. The new form of definition begins '**integer procedure**. . . ' , to show that it stands for an integer type value, and it 'gets the value out' by an assignment to the name. The effect on the main programme is rather breathtaking, as it *can* be written thus:

    begin integer procedure hcf (x,y);   **value** x,y;
      begin A: **if** x = y **then go to** Z;
          if x $\rangle$ y **then** x := x – y **else** y := y – x;
          go to A;   Z: hcf := x **end**;
      print(hcf(hcf(next, next), next)) **end**.

A more cautious programmer would retain a, b and c; nevertheless, on account of the value specification, each 'next' is only called once, and also in this problem the order of calling does not matter, with the result that certain possible traps do not materialize. When Algol is written in this style the result is very close to a function language.

An interesting field of speculation which we shall not follow up is what might have been done with the **perform** technique if parameters had been introduced *via* the lambda notation.

Overt recursion is explicitly permitted in Algol; that is, the following formulation, however inefficient, is valid:

> **integer procedure** hcf(x,y); **value** x,y;
> hcf := **if** x = y **then** x **else if** x ⟩ y **then**
> hcf (x – y,y) **else** hcf(x,y – x);

Implicit recursion also occurs in an expression like *hcf(hcf(a,b),c)* since (even on a call by value) the parameters are not evaluated before entering a routine but while in it, so that the evaluation of the inner *hcf* takes place *during* the evaluation of the outer one. (As implementation of recursion tends to be inefficient, a case can be made out for a variant of **procedure** — perhaps **function** — whose parameters may be evaluated before entry, in the old-fashioned way, whenever the system is such that time would be saved by doing so.)

11.2 Calling styles

A parameter of a procedure that is not called by value is said to be called *by name*. The principle of call by name was criticized by Strachey and Wilkes (1961) and an alternative, which they called 'call by simple name', was proposed, but in CPL they have incorporated all three types of call, under the titles of call by value, by reference (which is simple name) and by substitution (which is the Algol 'by name'). The distinction between these three may perhaps be best seen from the following very artificial example, which is written in Algol extended to admit all three types of call.

> **begin integer** i, **array** A[1:3]; **comment** this means that A has components A[1] .. A[3];
> **procedure** report (x, y, z); **value** x; **ref** y; **subs** z;
> **begin** i := 3;   A[1] := 5;   print(x, y, z) **end**
> i := 1;   A[1] := 2;   A[3] := 4;
> report(A[i], A[i], A[i]) **end**.

The result of this programme will be to print the numbers 2, 5, 4. In printing *x* the procedure has noted that *x* is *A[i]*, which was (at the moment of entry) *A[1]*, which had the value 2, and since *x* is called by value, this is what *x* remains, since no assignments in the form '*x* := . . .' occur. In printing *y*, the process stopped after determining the location referred to, and since *A[1]* is assigned the new value 5 before printing is called for, 5 is what is printed as the value of *y*. Finally, *z* remains *A[i]* up to the last minute, and therefore when it comes to printing it, it is interpreted as *A[3]*, which has the value 4. To avoid misunderstanding, we repeat that this example is in an extended Algol; in true Algol the first effect is obtained by the **value** specification, the third by refraining from writing this, and the second is not available.

90

Call by name is essential to the correct interpretation of the function $sigma(p(x),x,a,b)$ which we introduced earlier. The declaration of this function might be

```
real procedure sigma (p,q,r,s); value s;
    begin real S;
            S := 0;   q := r;
    Y:  if q > s then go to Z:
            S := S+p;   q := q+1;   go to Y;
    Z:  sigma := S end
```

We give s a value specification to avoid evaluating it (in case it is an expression) repeatedly at the statement Y. But p must be called by name or it will not vary as q is changed. This trick of making parameters functionally dependent on one another is known as the Jensen device. (Note that the two uses of p are completely independent, and do not lead to any clash.)

11.3 Higher level facilities

Like its immediate predecessors, Algol has a higher-level format for direct writing of loops. Unfortunately the official definitions are not sufficiently precise as to their effects when the distinctions between call by name and call by value are incorporated. The following statement incorporates all the possibilities in a 'for statement':

for i := a **step** b **until** c, d, e **while** f **do** X

There is a single controlled variable of numerical type, which is assigned values from a list separated by commas; these may be single values like d, or sequences like $a, a+b, a+2b \ldots$, or a single value such as e which is repeated until some condition occurs. However, this 'single' value need not be a 'constant' value. The expansion of the above statement in terms of simpler Algol is, according to the best authorities (Randell, 1963)

```
begin real j, k;   procedure Y; X;
        i := j := a;   k := b;
L:  if sign(k) × (c − j) ⩾ 0 then begin
        Y;   k := b; comment b may have been changed by Y;
        i := j := i+k;   go to L end;
        i := d;   Y;
M:  i := e;
        if f then begin Y; go to M end
end
```

In performing the expansion all expressions are replaced by name. Y replaces X here because in practice X may be very elaborate. The statement $i := j := i+k$ means that both i and j are to be set equal to $i + k$; in obeying this the order of evaluation is (i) address of i, (ii) address of j, (iii) address-thence-value of i, (iv) address-thence-value

91

of k, (v) value of $i+k$, and finally both assignments. The strictness and the inefficiency (in finding the address of i twice over) of this arises from the remote possibility that i might be a suffixed variable, whose suffix was defined by a subroutine which altered some of the values in i or elsewhere! It would normally be very bad programming technique if this occurred, but there are milder implications of call by name which must be allowed for, and the basic semantics of a language must give a definite ruling on the most outrageous things which it is possible to write. The above expansion does do this, and though it takes a clever compiler to know when it is safe to take a short cut, there are compilers which succeed in doing so.

Another feature which has proved more complex in elaborate situations than was originally envisaged is the declarator **own**. This can be applied to any local variable of a block and strictly speaking is not high-level since its effect cannot be reproduced in simpler Algol. Normally storage for local variables is raised on entry to the block (which may be a procedure body, of course) and relinquished on leaving it, but **own** preserves it until the next call. The effect of this is the same as declaring it globally except that (i) it cannot be referred to outside the block, and (ii) there is no need to check that it is notationally different from other global identifiers; complementary to (ii) is that in the case of library routines its declaration is inside them and one does not have to remember to add it. An example of its use would be in an iterative process used under circumstances where a working quantity of one application was a useful first approximation in the next. But its usefulness is greatly diminished by the lack of any method in Algol of initializing variables, so that one always has to take care that a first application of the routine does not call for an **own** variable while it is still void. More serious are the difficulties which arise in two less simple circumstances, (i) when the routine is called recursively, and (ii) in the case known as 'dynamic **own** arrays'. An example of the latter is the declaration '**own real array** A[n,n+3]'; suppose this to be called under circumstances in which n is alternately 0 and 1 — are the values of $A[0]$ and $A[4]$ to be lost or kept in cold storage when out of bounds? Landin (1965) has some remarks on the semantics of **own** which suggest that it would be sounder if the storage for an own variable 'sat' on a level with the declaration of the block, i.e. that in

begin . . . **begin real** x; **procedure** P; **begin own real** y . . .

y should not exist globally but come and go with x.

11.4 Criticisms
Discussion in the Algol Bulletin is very lively, and a survey of recent issues (July 1964—July 1965) shows a wide range of proposals for its improvement. The criticisms may be grouped under four heads:

1. Input/output
2. General problems which have arisen simply because Algol was the first language to pass a certain stage of sophistication
3. Effects of a narrowness of outlook, in that Algol is adapted almost exclusively to those computations describable as numerical analysis, and even here to treating vectors, etc, one component at a time
4. Its failure to recognize its own potentiality, in the sense that any well constructed Algol translator will handle correctly many natural but unauthorized extensions of Algol without difficulty.

As regards (1), the Algol 60 Report contains no proposals at all. It does 'recommend' that *sin, cos*, etc, as identifiers should be 'reserved' and usable without declaration (i.e. be system defined) and there is no difficulty in adding some input/output identifiers to this list. A great deal of the criticism under this head is invalidated by failure to appreciate the nuances implied by the word 'recommended', and for reasons which we detail in Section 14, we consider that the pressure from outside to force Algol to define exactly its *own* i/o arrangements is thoroughly misguided.

Under (4), there is no question but that the mechanism used to tie up a formal parameter with an actual parameter has the nature of 'assigning' a value to the formal parameter which could be used outside this context, and with this, if necessary, to qualify the semantics, any well constructed compiler should be able to handle the same range of types in free variables as in bound ones; applied to labels this would be far more useful than the switch (which is a favourite target for attack). Again, consider the following programme,

begin boolean B, C;   **real** x, y, z;
      real procedure val(f,g);   **real** g;   **procedure** f;   val := f(g);
      :
      z := val(**if** B **then** sin **else** cos, **if** C **then** x **else** y)

it seems unbelievable that a compiler which could interpret correctly the second parameter should fail over the first, yet the first is illegal Algol while the second is legal.

It would not be profitable to try to summarize the sort of proposals which are being made because (1) some will be described later in connection with younger languages, and (2) often the biggest problem concerns interrelations. Thus it is very important to introduce string variables and string handling functions but a string is a list of characters; similarly it is awkward if one cannot have *print*(x) and *print*(x,y) in the same programme, which one cannot because *print* must be declared with a determinate number of parameters — yet might not all procedures have just one parameter, a list? One comment may be used to sum up. Algol is, in fact, machine oriented in the sense that it recognizes that machines distinguish internally between fixed and

93

floating point operations but have to treat complex numbers as pairs of numbers with programmed arithmetic, and it bases its type discrimination on this fact, and not on the intrinsic computational properties of operands. In a similar way it recognizes that it defines an algorithm only to within the precision of the machine it is run upon, but ignores the computational fact that some calculations require some operands to be carried to greater precision than others (whatever their absolute length). Even so, it presented an enormous challenge to compiler-writers when first brought out, but this led to techniques which are now standard, and to new ideas in the organization of machines. This will be an iterative process.

12

LIST PROCESSING LANGUAGES

List processing languages arise (a) when the data structure is elaborate and has to be taken into account, but more importantly, (b) when this structure has to be operated upon as well as the values contained in it. (Were (a) the only reason, Cobol-type resources might well suffice.) The first work in this field began with Newell, Shaw and Simon in 1954 onwards, culminating in the 'Information Processing Language 5', or IPL-V, the manual for which appeared in 1961 (Newell, 1961). This work was directed towards simulating the 'more intelligent' types of computation, such as proving geometrical theorems in the Euclidean manner, or cybernetic simulation, and this aspect has all along proved a strong motivation for this type of language. IPL-V is a procedure language practically at the machine code level. In contrast, Lisp (McCarthy, 1960) is a function language. About the same time, Gelernter, Hansen and Gerberich (1960) published an extension of Fortran to accommodate lists, and Alp, a similar extension of Mercury Autocode, was announced two years later (Cooper and Whitfield, 1962). Slip (Weizenbaum, 1963) aimed at being embeddable in any existing procedural language, but was initially embedded in Fortran. Most recent is Wisp (Wilkes, 1964) — 'an experiment in a self-compiling compiler'; this is a system based initially on a simple but self-extending language, which is perhaps more comprehensible to conventional programmers than most of its predecessors. This brief history fails to do justice to a lot of work on list structure and list processing which did not result in a language whose name became known.

Many old hands will remember being asked at some time 'but can your machine solve an equation *algebraically*?' One always felt that the answer should be 'Yes, of course, if I could think how to write the programme'. It is list processing techniques which have shown how to programme a computer so that it can, for example, input a character string such as '$ax+b = cx+d$' and manipulate it so that it can be output in the rearranged form '$x = (d-b)/(a-c)$'.

In a list processing context, the external world to which a message refers is organized into *list-structures*, that is, *lists* which can be *lists of lists*. This is done by making each object in it consist of two parts (i) an intrinsic part and (ii) a pointer to the next object in the list, or, in the case of the last member of a list, a conventional termination. The intrinsic part can be either the value or the name of an object which represents the value. In the first case storage is saved but it also becomes inevitable that reference to any object can also be interpreted as reference to the list which it heads (which is only the same thing for the last member of a list).

12.1 Lisp notation

New types of object are bound to introduce new functional concepts, and, just as introduction of complex numbers forces one to augment the standard arithmetical functions with new ones such as 'real part', etc, so the introduction of lists forces the introduction of five or so new concepts and several other more convenient but less basic ones. The basic ones are usually referred to in the notation used in Lisp, and they are

A. Three functions of a single variable:
   1. $atom(x)$, a boolean function which is false if the value of x is a list, true otherwise;
   2. $car(x)$, which is what we have called the intrinsic part of x;
   3. $cdr(x)$, which is what we have called the pointer part of x;
B. Two functions of two variables
   4. $eq(x,y)$, a boolean which is true if x and y are the same atom, false if they are different atoms, and undefined if either of them is a list;
   5. $cons(x,y)$, which is the list z such that $car(z) = x$ and $cdr(z) = y$.

McCarthy also used the notations

$$(a \to b; c \to d; T \to e) \quad \text{and} \quad \text{cond}((a;b);(c;d);(T;e))$$

for

if a then b else if c then d else e

T being his notation for **true**. The origins of car and cdr are inconsequential; McCarthy partitioned a machine word which represented an object in the same way as it would have been partitioned had it been an instruction in machine code, and he used the same abbreviations (for 'content of address (or decrement) register') as were meaningful in the latter case. This is rather as though, because one originally had a machine designed to work in sterling, one always, when referring to the date, called months 'the shillings part of the date', but these names have caught on, and no rivals (such as *head* and *tail*, for example) would appear to have much chance against them. The concept of an atom is perhaps as relative as it is in physics; like the Algol black-type symbols, *car*, *cdr*, *cons*, etc, are atoms, but when it comes to numbers of more than one digit the choice is more open. Because arithmetic on numbers in pure list form is so inefficient, some compromise is necessary. Conversely, even the basic function names must be non-atomic to input/output routines.

Being a function language, Lisp gets by with the basic functions, although it finds certain abbreviations helpful, like *caar*(*x*) for *car* (*car*(*x*)). LAMBDA is an atom which performs the λ-operation. For exposition purposes Lisp is usually written with data in uppercase letters and the programme (i.e. the function) which is to be applied to the data in lowercase letters. But the latter is also a list structure and need not be expressed with a different, 'meta', set of symbols, and in a true Lisp programme the two are fed in using the same symbols, an atom APPLY serving to define the relation between 'programme' and 'data'. For recursive functions the transformation of Section 5.2.1 is used, Yλ appearing under the guise of LABEL — this word will soon have to be banned by mutual consent! Lisp presents the programmer accustomed to procedural languages with a very unfamiliar-looking problem — though we hope present readers may find Macrogenerator an introduction to this. A plain man's introduction to Lisp has been given by Woodward and Jenkins (1961).

12.2 Procedural List processing languages

When thinking procedurally about list processing, the functions of the previous section will be used in the way *sin*, *cos* and *log* are used in numerically oriented procedural languages. Certain other functions and objects are also so often used as to have acquired fairly universally used names. Storage which is not actually in use is kept on a 'free list', which we may call F. The following table takes the functions which Alp adds to Autocode and translates them into a form of Wisp. A few comments appear to be all that is necessary to clarify what must be, for some readers, a translation from one unfamiliar language into another unfamiliar one!

ALP	WISP	Comments
TO LIST(L,x)	CAR(L) = x	The first object in L is given the value *x*, overwriting previous contents.
FROM LIST(L,x)	x = CAR(L)	Converse of above (but see following text)
PUSHDOWN(L,x)	Z = F F = CDR(F) CDR(Z) = L CAR(Z) = x L = Z	A temporary name Z is needed. The first object in F is detached from it, given the value *x*, and then put on the front of *L*.
POP UP(L,x)	x = CAR(L) Z = L L = CDR(L) CDR(Z) = F F = Z	Converse of above. The Wisp translation omits a branch on IF CDR(L) = 0, in case *L* is already the last object.
INSERT AFTER(L,x)	Z = F F = CDR(F) CDR(Z) = CDR(L) CDR(L) = Z CAR(Z) = x	The first object in F is detached and inserted into the second place of *L* and then given the value *x*.

LINK(L,M,R)	TO R IF CDR(L) = O M = CDR(L)	M now names the tail of L; if L has no tail, control is transferred to R.
SETLINK(L,M)	CDR(L) = M	I.e. L = CONS(CAR(L),M)
NEWCELL(L)	L = F F = CDR(F)	The first object on F is removed and called L.
ERASE(L)	Z = L R: TO S IF CDR(Z) = O Z = CDR(Z) TO R S: CDR(Z) = F F = L	Simplified by assuming that L is unbranched. Returns the whole of L to F. (See note below on labels)
FIND(L,M,R,x)	M = L S: TO T IF CAR(M) = x TO R IF CDR(M) = O M = CDR(M) TO S T:	Finds first object on L which refers to x, leaving its name in M; in case of none, leaves name of last object of L in M and transfers control to R.
ADDSPACE(a,b)	(None)	Concerned with setting up a free list when first going from Autocode to list working.

In this table both languages have been adapted slightly to each other both in notation and semantics. In Wisp, for example, the arguments of *car* and *cdr* are written without brackets, and labels are integers on a line to themselves, not alphanumeric with a colon. Considerable liberty has been taken with the variable x; in Alp x is a complex of three 'fields' whose interpretation is dependent on the usual Autocode conventions in integer and real variables, etc, while in Wisp it does not really exist at all. This is because Wisp was designed as a compiler writing aid, and admits only single characters or lists as values; hence the true Wisp equivalent to the first Alp instruction is one of the three forms

> CAR L = M   The value of the first object in L is made equal to the name of the list M
> CAR L = M: The value of the first object in L is made equal to the character 'M'
> CAR L = CAR M   The value of the first object in L is made equal to the value of the first object in M

and the second Alp instruction is now already covered by the last of these three. In Alp the pre-existence of the Autocode variables is assumed, and they play the part for which we shall see that 'data-terms' are introduced into IPL-V. The data-terms of Wisp are all single characters, and the more economic storage scheme is practicable.

12.3 IPL-V

IPL-V is the assembly code of a hypothetical machine, and, like most list processing languages in the current state of the art, it is interpreted, not translated. The store of this hypothetical machine is, of course, the store of the actual machine less that part taken up by the interpretive system, and at the start of a programme it is arranged to suit the problem by setting aside certain locations as named list-heads, and putting the remainder on to a free-list. (Contrast the more limited facilities of Wisp which has single letters only as list-head names and therefore no need for preliminary setting). Such a list-head name is known as a *regional symbol*, and consists outside the machine of a letter (or punctuation mark) followed by an integer. All symbols with the same letter are said to belong to the same region, and the setting up is done by means of directives which state the maximum integer used in each region, and possibly its starting point in the store. Synonyms can be arranged by making the regions overlap. Regions H, J and W have preset size and purposes which will appear. Besides regional symbols there are also *local symbols*, of the form 9-⟨integer⟩ (e.g. '9–12'), which retain a fixed meaning only within a given list-structure starting at a regionally defined head. Internally, all symbols are machine addresses, combined with a prefix to distinguish regional, local and anonymous symbols (the last derived usually by transfers from the free list).

Being at the assembly code level, a programme consists of a series of 'lines' equivalent either to a machine word plus a label, or to a directive. We can expand this to

⟨line⟩ ::= ⟨preamble⟩ ⟨machine word⟩
⟨preamble⟩ ::= ⟨type⟩⟨label⟩⟨sign⟩
⟨machine word⟩ ::= ⟨P⟩⟨Q⟩⟨car⟩⟨cdr⟩|⟨P⟩⟨Q⟩⟨value⟩

where

⟨type⟩ is an octal digit, zero or blank except in directives. We shall denote a line whose type is n by ⟨n-line⟩.
⟨sign⟩ is blank except on numerical values, or as a means of distinguishing data items in instruction lists.
⟨P⟩ and ⟨Q⟩ are octal digits known as the prefix.

Since the system was designed for card input, on which syntactical units occupy fixed columns, blank causes no trouble. The units ⟨label⟩, ⟨car⟩ and ⟨cdr⟩ are all symbols or blank; in the case of ⟨label⟩ a blank implies that the symbol is an address removed from the free list during input, in the other two cases a blank implies the label of the next line.

A complete programme has the structure

⟨programme⟩ ::= ⟨controls⟩⟨mainpart⟩⟨endline⟩
⟨controls⟩ ::= ⟨9-line⟩|⟨controls⟩⟨region control line⟩
⟨endline⟩ ::= ⟨5-line blank except for the label of the entry
             point in ⟨symbol⟩⟩
⟨mainpart⟩ ::= ⟨block⟩|⟨block⟩⟨mainpart⟩
⟨block⟩ ::= ⟨5-line⟩⟨list sequence⟩

On the whole, data and instructions are kept in separate blocks, being distinguished by ⟨Q⟩ = 1 or 0 respectively in the 5-line of the

99

block. The structure $\langle P \rangle \langle Q \rangle \langle car \rangle \langle cdr \rangle$ is known as a list-cell and the structure $\langle P \rangle \langle Q \rangle \langle value \rangle$ as a data-term. The latter obtains (a) when $\langle Q \rangle$ has the value '1' and the item occurs within a data block, or (b) when the $\langle sign \rangle$ is not blank; values 0 . . . 3 of $\langle P \rangle$ then cause it to be interpreted as decimal integer, floating point number, alphanumeric or octal quantity, respectively. Case (b) will apply to 'programme constants' and the item will need a local symbol to be referenced by. In case (a) it must have a regional symbol as its label, thus appearing under the guise of a single membered list. True lists in data blocks have a label, followed on the *next* and succeeding lines by '$\langle Q \rangle = 0$' lines whose *car*'s are either the names of data terms or the names of other lists. (In many applications of IPL-V it is assumed that the list is a list of objects, and that the *car* of the *initial* line is the name of a list of properties associated with the objects.) The last line in any list has a zero *cdr*. IPL-V imposes certain restrictions on the input of data lists which, for example, bar circular lists. Some of these restrictions can be overridden during the subsequent operation of the programme.

In instruction lists, each word is an instruction unless a sign has been punched, $\langle P \rangle$ being the function, $\langle Q \rangle \langle car \rangle$ the operand (denoted by 'S') and $\langle cdr \rangle$ the 'next instruction source'. The $\langle Q \rangle$ part of the operand determines whether the $\langle car \rangle$ part is to be taken literally, its value to be used, or (when its value is in turn a symbol) the value of its value. The eight codes for $\langle Q \rangle$ are

0   'Execute' or 'obey'. S must be the label either of a subroutine or of one of the nearly two hundred machine order sequences in region J.
1   Pushdown(HO,S)
2   Pop up(HO,S)
3   Pop up(S, S)   i.e. destroying top contents
4   Pushdown(S, S)   i.e. duplicating top contents
5   To list(HO, S)
6   From list(HO,S)
7   Branch to S if H5 holds '-'

The head cell of list HO is known as the 'communication cell' and plays a ubiquitous role resembling that of the accumulator of an ordinary machine, but being the head of a pushdown list it can hold an indefinite amount of information, and parameters of routines, irrespective of their number, are handed over in it. Thus the nearest simple equivalent to Alp's FIND would be a sequence to find the first list cell (other than the head) in *L2* (say) which has *X3* as its *car*, leaving its name in *MO* or, if there is none, leaving the name of the last cell in *MO* and jumping to *R1*. Routine *J62* is defined thus:

A search of list with name (1) is made, testing each symbol against (0) (starting with the cell after cell (1)). If (0) is found, the output

100

(0) is the name of the cell containing it and $H5$ is set +.... If (0) is not found, the output (0) is the name of the last cell on the list, and $H5$ is set -.

Here (0), (1) ... refer to the top, next ... cells in HO. So the coding is

P	Q	car	cdr	Comments
1	0	L2		Push name of $L2$ into $H0$
1	0	X3		And name of X3
0	0	J62		Obey $J62$
2	0	MO		Pop up $H0$ to $M0$
7	0	R1		Branch on content of $H5$.

ERASE(L) can be treated similarly using $J71$, which erases the list named in (0), or $J72$, which erases the list structure, i.e. the list and all its *locally defined* sub-lists.

It will be clear that at this point there is a barrier to any further discussion of this language unless we are prepared to reprint the complete specifications of all the routines in the J region.

12.4 Future develoments

The day of list processing languages would seem to be over. They have served their purpose in isolating for study the features required for facile handling of lists, and these are now being included in general purpose languages, not as added grafts, but as an integral part of the language from the moment of its inception.

13
C.P.L. AND THE IBM SHARE ISSUE

At the moment of writing, two languages have appeared which belong to a new generation, and whose impact and worth have still to be assessed. These are CPL and PL/I. Superficially, the former looks like a new Algol with acknowledgments to the necessity for lists, and the latter like a new Fortran with acknowledgments to Cobol, but in both cases the sponsors have been at pains to emphasize that they have, in fact, made a completely new start. As both languages have been introduced by an excellent article in advance of the issue of manuals (Barron *et al*, 1963; Radin and Rogoway, 1965), which any attempt to summarize the languages separately could only duplicate, we shall consider them together.

13.1 Immediate impressions
And surely the first comment called for is that both languages have made an unfortunate start in the matter of their names? The current practice in some publications of always using block capitals for language names like ALGOL or COBOL — a distinction denied to names such as Sanskrit or Washington or Churchill — serves only to betray the stage of adolescent arrogance which is all our subject seems as yet to have attained, and a choice of names which cannot be written in a normal way simply perpetuates this forcing of ugliness on to the printed page. CPL is an abbreviation of 'Combined Programming Language — or possibly 'Cambridge Plus London', since it is a joint effort of the computing departments of these two universities. PL/I is short for 'Programming Language No. 1' — a name which replaced NPL (for 'New Programming Language') after protests from the National Physical Laboratory — and is the product of a team set up by the Share organization of Fortran users. Both NPL and PL/I slightly suggest an attitude of 'sell it on its name if it won't sell on its merits '— which is misleading as the merits are there all right even if they do need supplementing. Comparison of CPL and PL/I will reveal complementary strengths and weaknesses which lead one to hope that any political struggle between them will result in stalemate.

The superficial impressions already referred to are created mainly, though not entirely, by the character sets used. It is unfortunate that neither team looked ahead sufficiently to employ the I.S.O. standard character set, but this is not serious, since neither language would find it difficult to free itself from the historical associations which have determined its present form. CPL is based on the Flexowriter set, including backspacing for underlining and for some other over-printing (e.g. $\neq$ from $=$ and $/$), and thus can draw on a large set of characters; it actually uses 149 (or 123 allowing for the fact that underlined ($=$ heavy type) *letters* are semantically the same whether in upper or lowercase). PL/I allows any character set the equipment is capable of in data, and therefore in constants within a programme, but its syntactic requirements are met in terms of a restricted set based on old style card practice — 60 characters in all, with certain fixed conventions for making do with 48 when necessary. Although a large number of keywords are used — words with defined syntactic and semantic properties — none of these are reserved (i.e. unusable in other senses) except those which alternate for characters and character combinations not available in the 48-character set.

A second major contribution to the superficial impression comes from the syntactical form adopted for statement brackets. Whereas in Algol **begin** and **end** are *symbols* with the properties of brackets, in Fortran the corresponding objects are *statements*, and this divergence of usage persists. Both sides can claim precedents in natural languages; compare

1. According to his letter 'violence may be necessary'.
2. According to his letter, and I quote, violence may be necessary. (Quote ends.)

Preference here is probably personal, but there can be no doubt that the occurrence of words like PROCEDURE and DO followed immediately by a semicolon is a deep-rooted source of the superficial impression.

13.2 Methods of approach

The two sponsoring bodies seem to have had quite different methods of approach to their task, the Americans aiming at a complete specification of the language prior to any compiler writing, while the British team used the process of compiler writing as a sub-process of defining the language.

In fact, London and Cambridge independently undertook the writing of a compiler — the former on rather traditional lines and the latter on the basis of Landin's theory of applicative expressions. They arranged to meet frequently in order to ensure that no divergent interpretations developed. This, when it can be afforded, is an excellent way of approaching the semantics of a new language. It has been said of certain languages in the past that their only true semantics were what their originator's compiler made them do on the

103

machine for which it was written. This has often meant that interpretation of obscurer points was based on how the first compiler found it easiest to approach less obscure related points, and not on what the notation was most likely to mean in the hands of the first programmer to try to use it. With two independent compilers being produced in collaboration, any conflict of the form 'my compiler makes it mean this but your compiler makes it mean that' is resolved by both parties forgetting their own compilers and asking 'what will a user be most likely to think it means?' and/or 'what ought it to mean?'. (*Prima facie* it ought to mean what it seems to mean, but occasionally this might lead to two ways of saying one thing and no way of saying another, in which case the doubtful expression 'ought' perhaps to take the second meaning.) There is one respect, however, in which the impact of the two-compiler approach has been weakened; it would have been stronger had the two universities not possessed computers which are practically identical so far as their central processors are concerned — see, for example, the remarks later on precision.

By contrast, the Americans issued a series of three language specifications, the first two being drafts circulated for comment. For our purposes — comparative study — the earlier reports are no less valuable than the final one. The first proposed a sort of contemporary-style union of Fortran and Cobol which nevertheless failed to prevent the traditions of the parent languages from being a drag — e.g. there was a limit on the number of subscripts which a variable could have. The second showed a much healthier approach while still planning for the present rather than for the future. The proposals in the third report, while containing a rather complete and sound coverage for most present needs, also contain a few features with implications too far-reaching to be seen immediately. At last the lesson which the Algol committee unconsciously taught has been learned; that to win its way a new language must be easy and safe to use at an elementary level, and must arouse controversy at an advanced level!

There also seems to have been a divergence of opinion as to the sort of improvements which ought to be included in a new language. The Americans have gone all out for a simple and unified syntax capable of comprehending all those processes which had to be tortuously expressed in earlier languages, but they have concentrated on doing more easily those things which are already common practice, not on increasing the range. The British have aimed at increasing — in a sense, in completing — the semantic coverage so as to offer new facilities, and confessedly have treated syntax as window-dressing. Possibly this represents commercial/university rather than national temperamental contrast; a language for use by conservative customers as against one for use by adventuresome students. Or there may be a contrast between domination by people who compute and

104

domination by people who make and sell computers. And one can speculate on the most outstanding exception to this generalization — that PL/I makes full provision for parallel processing, whereas CPL, apparently, does not.

13.3 Detailed objectives

The objectives of the PL/I team, as set out by Radin and Rogoway, were six in number. (1) Nothing to be illegal which makes clear and unambiguous sense. (2) As far as possible it should never be necessary to escape into machine code. (3) Independence of machine characteristics. (4) 'Modularity.' (5) 'Catering to the novice.' (6) Aprogramming, not an algorithmic language. The aim in CPL, as described in Barron *et al*, was 'to produce a language which could be used for all types of problem, numerical and non-numerical, and (which) would allow programmers to exploit all the facilities of a large and powerful computer without having to escape into machine code . . . to a large extent based on Algol (so far as "syntactic sugar" is concerned)'. Thus CPL subscribes to PL/I's 'Objective 2' in almost identical words. 'Objective 1' it took for granted, since though not realized in either Fortran or Cobol, it was already a principle in Algol; the pity is that PL/I have so often paid it no more than lip service, as we shall see from time to time. Though not in the passage quoted above, CPL also endorses PL/I's 'Objective 6', but apparently with a different interpretation; to PL/I this seems to mean primarily that the language must cater for terminal equipment, but to CPL that it must recognize that multi-length working is sometimes necessary. The latter is the question of precision; it is tied up with PL/I's 'Objective 3' and gets fuller consideration later. There may be some virtue in the former as regards equipments of types which are, one hopes, obsolescent. But apart from this, for reasons which are scattered throughout this book, we cannot recognize the distinction, holding that if a language is a bad programming language on either of these grounds, then it is *ipso facto* an equally bad algorithmic language.

Under 'Objectives 4 and 5', PL/I is designed so that subsets of it for particular purposes can be used in ignorance of other parts of it, and this need cost nothing in compilation or running time. Default interpretations are provided for all declarations not explicitly made, and redundant forms of commonly used cases of otherwise complex usages are provided.

'Modularity' is also used in another sense, namely, the preservation of what Fortran always claimed as a virtue, that already compiled routines could be incorporated in a programme as separate modules without recompilation. The original virtue of modularity in this sense appeared in a context of slow compilation to a fast-running object programme. Its cost is that a global variable cannot be declared globally but must be redeclared in every routine that uses it

105

(so that each such routine can be compiled independently of the others) and that some efficient mechanism must be provided for establishing correct references to actual global storage during the final compilation when the modules are brought together. Today it is at least as important to assess it in terms of how library and other backing store facilities are to be handled. When a programme is compiled at a single go, inner routines will always be more efficient if they refer directly to a global variable than if they refer to it by a parameter mechanism, but in Algol the latter was the only method available to routines stored in a library. However, there seems no reason why a parameter mechanism should not, in appropriate cases, be as efficient as the linking mechanism required by modularity. At all events CPL does not seem to have considered modularity worth incorporating, although it is curious that it does not even include an equivalent to the Cobol COPY facility; possibly it is held that this should be done by a pre-compilation process (from a meta-CPL into true CPL) under control of a systems programme, or it may be buried in the implications of the file concept.

The principle that redundant syntax shall be provided has been carried much further by CPL than by PL/I. In the latter, for example, it is true that while all sixteen boolean functions of two variables are provided by the notation BOOL(X,Y,Z) where Z is the contents of the 2×2 table (for XY = 00, 01, 10, 11) defining the function, the commoner functions such as 'X&Y' are also available in the infixed-operator form. But this has two purposes; while it does ease things for beginners, it also aids direct (and therefore more efficient) coding on any machine possessing the '&' function. And the over-all syntax of the language is unaffected by this duplication, except by the addition of '&' to some list of operators. In CPL, however, an attempt has been made to validate any natural syntactic variation in the method of describing a given process. To some extent this is application of the process of natural development described in Section 2.1, since it means incorporating so many of those things one does with Algol when merely scribbling first drafts — **unless** and **until**, for example, as alternatives to **if** and **while** to save a **not**(. . .), and the use of more compact brackets (§ and §) in place of **begin** and **end**. In principle, any variation which is natural and unambiguous goes — in practice, provided enough people find it natural to make it worth forcing the compiler to recognize it, of course — so that the following are all equivalent, the differences serving to cater for personal preference or for one's feeling for the English language:

> **test** B **then** apply **or** convert
> **test** B **then do** application **or** conversion
> **test** B **do** application **or** conversion
> **if**   B **then** apply; **unless** B **do** convert

106

But **if** and **test** are not equivalent; the ambiguity problems into which Algol ran are eliminated by distinguishing in this way whether one or both alternatives are explicit.

PL/I's 'Objective 1' is quite different, although also a form of 'anything goes'; it implies no increase in syntactic freedom, but requires that everything syntactically valid shall, if possible, be semantically valid as well, and certainly not arbitrarily ruled out because of current difficulties of implementation. It is a perpetual challenge because it means that every new feature of a developing language must be validated, not only by itself, but also in every syntactically possible combination with all previously existing features of the language unless semantically absurd. For example, IF X THEN . . . is absurd if X is a floating-point number, but $Z = X+Y$ is not absurd if X is a character string currently all numeral (or even containing a decimal point or sign character).

13.4 General syntax

Because of the contention, in CPL, that syntax is a superficial matter, the general syntax of CPL is relatively uninteresting. Care has been taken, however, to see that no structure is held in common with Algol unless its semantics are the same — see, in particular, the syntax and semantics of **for** below. In PL/I, a programme consists of 'modules' which can be compiled separately. Each module is an 'external procedure' constructed from units which are one of the following:

in PL/I	corresponding to Algol's
simple statements	simple statements
compound statements	conditional statements
DO groups	compound and 'for' statements
BEGIN blocks	blocks
'internal procedures'	procedure declarations

Owing to the unfortunate confusion which this can raise concerning the use of the word 'compound', we shall replace it, in discussing PL/I, by 'complex' — using this word in the grammarian's sense, not the mathematician's. Internal and external procedures are identical syntactically but differ semantically in that in the absence of explicit declarations of the variables they use, the latter fall back on default conventions whereas the former accept the declarations of the containing procedure. The 'main programme' is an external procedure which has a declared attribute MAIN. Every simple statement starts with a verb which determines its class, except for assignment statements, which take the conventional form (e.g. $X = Y = 2$;); note that '$=$' is the imperative, EQ being used for the relational operator. Although this resembles the approach in Cobol, PL/I achieves a much more uniform treatment of the syntax of the various classes of

107

statement, on account of (a) its natural incorporation of mathematical symbolism, and (b) its use of the 'attribute' concept.

13.5 Some miscellaneous points

Certain features common to both languages may be listed as indicating trends towards desirable conventions in language development generally. Many of them tie in with conventions already established in natural languages. (1) Both use an identifier followed by a full colon to indicate a label (natural in English and *ex* Algol, but an innovation to the Fortran tradition). (2) Both languages make provision for assigning an initial value to a variable when declaring it. (3) Both give a semantic significance to 'at least one space' while denying it to page layout in general. CPL adds to this that while semicolons separate statements within lines, one will be assumed at the end of a line whenever it is syntactically appropriate, thus eliminating the possibility of what is the most frequent *careless* mistake in Algol, and providing another example of 'what is natural will be provided for'. (4) The operators $\times$, $/$, $\div$ and 'to the power' ($\uparrow$ in CPL and ** in PL/I) are of equal precedence and associate from right to left, while $+$ and $-$ are less binding and associate from left to right; this gives strings such as a/bc their most natural interpretation. (5) Both languages agree about the principle of labelling brackets and short-circuiting their closure, although the techniques are somewhat different. In Algol one can find oneself writing sequences like

A: **begin** . . . B: **begin** . . . C: **begin** . . . **end** C **end** B **end** A;

but the C, B and A following the **ends** rank as comment. Such comments help one to count up the number of statements brackets which need closing. Both of the languages we are now considering agree that under these circumstances the compiler can do the counting, and that ' . . . **end** A;' should make it redundant (though not wrong, of course) to write the inner **ends**. PL/I adopts almost exactly this technique, while CPL, instead of using labels for the purpose, allows 'section and subsection type' numbering of statement brackets, thus

$\S\, 4.2 \ldots \S\, 4.2.1 \ldots \S\, 4.2$

where $\S\, 4.2$ implies a preceding $\S\, 4.2.1$ if an explicit one has not already occurred.

Other moves by CPL to bring its notation into accord with algebraic convention are to allow any identifier to conclude with any number of primes, and to restore implicit representation of multiplication by juxtaposition. Multi-character identifiers must start with a capital letter, and, if multiplied implicitly, be separated from the next by a space. Thus

bb $-$ 4ac
a''a'' $-$ 4a'a'''
Second $\uparrow$ 2 $-$ 4 First Third

108

are all possible ways of expressing the discriminant of a quadratic. However, according to this rule, the trigonometric functions must be given capital letters. Also, round brackets are kept strictly for sub-expressions, and square ones used for *both* subscripts and parameter lists — a move which is very logical but definitely away from established conventions.

Matters like this are unattainable luxuries to PL/I, which, as the variations from the first report to the third show, has had a certain difficulty in constraining itself within the limited character set it has allowed itself. One area in which this has happened is illustrated by

> In Report 1, identifiers may be up to eight alphanumeric characters (letters or numerals); structures are introduced but their nomenclature is inadequately described.
>
> In Report 2, any number of alphanumeric characters may be used and the period is allowed internally so as to provide e.g. RATE.OF. PAY as a single identifier. For Cobol's MONTH IN MASTER, the construction MASTER $ MONTH is laid down.
>
> In Report 3, up to 31 (*sic*) alphanumerics are allowed, with RATE_ OF_PAY as a single identifier, and MASTER.MONTH as the method of referring to an element in a structure. But the break character (the _) has no equivalent in the 48-character set, and with this set one has to fall back on RATEOFPAY.

Neither language has had the courage to insist, against the conservatism of the equipment manufacturers, on distinct opening and closing quotes, so that both fall back on the clumsy system whereby alternate quotes are openers and closers and a special notation is required for nested quotes. In PL/I this is '' (so that '''' means ''). In CPL, | is used as an escape character within quotes, so that not only are || and |' the in-quote representations of | and ', but |n and |t provide 'newline' and 'tab' symbols, and so on. Outside quotes, || introduces comment and is cancelled by the end of the line; in PL/I comment took the form // ... // in Report 1, and became /* ... */ in Reports 2 and 3. Once digraph characters are introduced, one wonders why nobody has done the logical thing and used brackets throughout for all purposes which are logically brackets, e.g. (' ... ') for quotes and (* ... *) for comment and similarly for any other paired symbols that may be required (as in Macrogenerator, for example). (The alternative '(...)' and *(...)* is almost impossible to reconcile with other usages such as * as an infixed operator.)

13.5.1 Side effects and conditionals

On the controversial question of side effects, CPL sets its face uncompromisingly against them in functions. This is, of course, a flat repudiation of the objective of allowing programmers 'to exploit *all* the facilities of a large and powerful computer without having to escape into machine code'. It is not easy to say whether this is sheer prejudice (in an age when most of physics rests on the relation $pq - qp \neq 0$), or is due to the exigencies of the applicative expression approach. If it is the latter then it may be forgiven, since this is an important advance in the direction of formal semantics. The attitude of PL/I is more liberal and sensible; functions are presumed not to have side effects and procedures are assumed to have them *in default of a declaration to the contrary*. A declaration that a function has side effects will inhibit optimizing rearrangements of the order of evaluation of the parts of an expression containing it — selectively if necessary. (Such rearrangements may also nullify a programmer's intentions with regard to round-off, and CPL has not avoided having to provide means to inhibit them when necessary.)

Non-controversial, but a trouble spot in Algol, was the problem of keeping conditionals unambiguous. CPL has dealt with this by (1) using McCarthy's notation for conditional expressions, and (2) restricting **if** and **unless** to the form of conditional statement without **else**, replacing **if** by **test** in the case when both alternatives are explicit. An example which includes most of the possibilities (and complicated enough to be difficult reading in any language) is

if a$\rangle$b → B1, B2 **then do test** B3 **then do** X **or do** p := B4 → 1,
B5 → 2, 3

The **or** must belong to the **test** and not to the **if.** The Algol equivalent to this makes easier reading with a few redundant brackets, but without them it is

if if a$\rangle$b **then** B1 **else** B2 **then begin if** B3 **then** X
else p := **if** B4 **then** 1 **else if** B5 **then** 2 **else** 3 **end**

The PL/I solution (in the 48-character set) would seem to be

IF (A GT B)*B1+(A LE B)*B2 THEN IF B3 THEN CALL X;
ELSE P = B4+(NOT B4)*(2*B5+3*(NOT B5));

in which the final expression might, under certain circumstances, be optimized to $P = 3 - 2*B4 - B5 + B4*B5$. It depends on (a) use of 1 and 0 for **true** and **false**, which we discuss later, (b) the rule that an ELSE always pairs with the nearest unpaired IF, and (c) the quaint consequences of the syntax of complex statements and the use of statements as statement brackets. The semicolon ends a simple statement, rather than, as in some languages, separating statements. The complex statement-forms end with simple statements and thus end with semicolons, but not in their own right. In Report 2 an attempt was made to get rid of THEN, which was possible because of the limited meaning of the space. If this was an attempt to get closer to English usage, it was a mistake, because although many English if-sentences omit 'then', the majority of those that do have a comma where it would have been, and the effect of the omission on clarity was

110

deplorable. It led to strings like *IF B X = Y*, for *IF B THEN X = Y* (or *IF B, X = Y*). Even as it is, we are saddled with curiosities like

IF A THEN IF B THEN X = Y; ELSE; ELSE X = 0;

Here the final semicolon is part of 'X = 0;', and the middle one is a dummy statement, the alternative to 'X = Y;' for use when B has the value **false** (= 0). The sequence

IF A THEN DO; IF B THEN X = Y; END; ELSE X = 0;

is equivalent, both make X = 0 the 'A is false' branch. But

IF A THEN IF B THEN X = Y; ELSE X = 0;

is different, since the ELSE attaches itself to the most recent un-matched IF, so that this is a dummy when A is false. In all three statements X = Y results when both A and B are true.

13.6 Types

When we turn to the question of 'types' we find evidence of the un-settled state of our present knowledge in this area, as well as of the different viewpoints of the two teams. The Share team has clearly had commercial requirements more in the forefront of their minds than the CPL team had. Both enter a caveat that early implementations may be confined to a subset, and in the case of CPL this may have the effect of leaving the answers to some questions still open.

In CPL the three plenipotent types from Algol, viz., **integer, real** and **boolean,** have been supplemented by **complex, string, logical** and **label.** The Algol *string* and *label* types, that is, have been promoted to full status, and *complex* and *logical* have been added. The latter treats a word simply as a string of bits. An integer with suitable pro-perties may alternatively be designated **index** if storing it in an index register will help the compiler to produce a more efficient programme. **General** is available to describe a variable which will not take on a definite type until later — possibly only at run time, and possibly changing during the run. A machine word (whatever that may be in a given implementation) is standard, and only lengths related to this are provided for. Integer, real and complex may be **double** length, and logical, normally half length, may be **long logical.** There is no pro-vision for 'complex integers'. For non-scalar quantities, **array** and **list** are available. Array bounds must be declared but lists are true list structures; there is no provision for structure handling in the Cobol sense. The list of types is not regarded as necessarily closed.

In the initial implementation at London the only form of declara-tion is

let ⟨compound definition⟩⟨;⟩

where ⟨;⟩ is an actual or assumed semicolon, although in Barron *et al* the Algol syntax (i.e. ⟨type⟩⟨id.list⟩⟨;⟩) seems also to be envisaged.

The expansion of ⟨compound definition⟩ is in two stages. First, the productions

⟨cpd def⟩ ::= ⟨mul def⟩ **and** ⟨cpd def⟩|⟨mul def⟩
⟨mul def⟩ ::= ⟨where def⟩ **in** ⟨mul def⟩|⟨where def⟩
⟨where def⟩ ::= ⟨def⟩ $0 {**where** ⟨def⟩}

define how compound definitions are built up from simple ones, and secondly five types of simple definition are shown. These are

1. ⟨rec⟩⟨§⟩⟨cpd def⟩⟨§⟩

which allows a compound definition in statement brackets (with identifying tags if desired) to function as a simple definition.

2. ⟨id.list⟩ ↑ 1 **all** {**be**| **is**| **are**} ⟨type list⟩

which is the equivalent of an Algol declaration. Note the concession to 'let x be . . . ' but 'where x is . . . ' . Next

3. ⟨id.list⟩{=| ≃ | ≡}⟨expression list⟩

which provides declaration with initialization. Finally

4. ⟨rec⟩ **routine** ⟨identifier⟩⟨par.list⟩⟨spec.list⟩⟨command⟩

is the equivalent of an Algol procedure declaration and

5. ⟨rec⟩ ↑ 1{⟨type⟩**func**| **func**}⟨identifier⟩⟨par.list⟩⟨=⟩⟨expression⟩

of an Algol function-designator declaration. A declaration (other than one following **where**) becomes operative at the beginning of the *next* declaration (or statement) if ⟨rec⟩ is ⟨empty⟩, but at the beginning of the declaration in which it stands if ⟨rec⟩ is **rec**. Thus **rec** has a more general function than that of merely pointing out that a function is recursive. To revive the old question of dynamic array bounds (and to presume on the notation for declaring bounds), of

1. **let** n = 5;   **let** A = Newarray[**real**, (l,n)]
2. **let rec** §n = 5 **and** A = Newarray[**real**, (l,n)]§
3. **let** n = 5 **and** A = Newarray[**real**,(l,n)]

the first two are valid but the third, unless there is a prior declaration of and assignment to *n*, is not. In an example like this, the type of *n* is that of the right-hand side, a preferred type being selected if this is numerical; this can be changed during the message by writing, e.g. **prefer real**. The ⟨=⟩ in (5) will, in later implementations, include all three variants shown in (3), which imply that the free variables in the expression are called by value, reference or substitution, respectively (see Section 11.2). The ⟨spec.list⟩ in (4) contains only the call specifications, type specification being in the parameter list, thus:

let routine R[**real** x, y, **label** L]**val** x, **ref** y **be** § . . §

The ⟨spec.list⟩ is omitted from (5) because, to prevent side effects, all parameters of a function are automatically called by value. (Omission of an optional **be** from (4) is an implementation discrepancy.)

It would also seem to be an implementational discrepancy that ↑1 **all** is omitted from (3). It is a semantic requirement in both (2) and

112

(3) that either (1) **all** is omitted and the two lists are of the same length, or (2) **all** is included and the second list is single-membered. I.e. let *a,b,c = 0,0,0* or let *a,b,c* **all** = *0*. This situation occurs again in assignment statements (see Section 13.11).

In their earlier reports the Share committee allowed for nine options for the type of a scalar, FIXED (point), FLOAT(ing point), COMPLEX, LOGICAL (i.e. with values TRUE and FALSE), CHAR (acter string), BIT (string), LABEL, PROCEDURE VARIABLE and FILE VARIABLE, the last three being known as 'address types'. Broadly the first seven of these correspond with those of CPL. However, the first three of these can have a *precision* attribute specified after them in brackets, a system-defined precision being assumed only by default; the string types *must* have *lengths* specified in the same way (or, in the case of CHAR by a picture), though (*) can indicate that the specification has been made elsewhere when the variable is EXTERNAL (see later), and VARIABLE means that the length specified is only a maximum. In the final version, LOGICAL has been deleted, the character and bit string types remain, and numerical types may be specified independently as fixed/float, binary/decimal and real/complex — eight variations of 'numerical' in all. Note that FIXED is not INTEGER: a precision (3.2) means three significant figures, two after the decimal point.

The specification of precision in PL/I is in accord with the objective of making a programme machine-independent, but one may assume that when default precision is used this will usually be the precision of a machine word and that this is bound to lead to a more efficient object programme. If default is used to get efficiency in this way then there is no way of asking for double precision in those cases where the numerical analysis requires it for certain variables, other than knowing the precision of the system at single length. In CPL, on the other hand, precision is an inescapable function of the system.

Abolition of LOGICAL as a separate type is a natural consequence of being able to specify a variable as a one-bit string, and numerical interpretation of this is natural to most machines. Furthermore, the provision of a complete and well-defined set of transfer functions is necessary to achieve 'Objective 1' (since there can be no doubt what a programmer means when he multiplies something by the *character string* 3.14159), and the advantages of being able to use logical variables in an arithmetic way are undoubtedly great. Nevertheless one must have reservations about the wisdom of this move, primarily on one ground. This is that in evaluating an expression such as $B1 \rightarrow x, B2 \rightarrow y, T \rightarrow z$, if $B1$ has the value **true** then no attempt is made to evaluate any of the quantities $B2$, y, z. Consequently such an expression is valid when $B1$ is **true** and x fully defined, even though $B2$, y or z may be void, unsited, or even (if this is possible) not yet declared. Under these circumstances a purely arithmetic interpretation

113

can lead to trouble unless (a) the boolean is always the first factor and (b) if it is zero the second is not evaluated; certainly an optimization like $P = 3 - 2*B4 - B5 + B4*B5$ cannot be permitted. Default initialization covers a large proportion of difficult cases but not all. In particular, if *B2* has side effects they must not be excited when *B1* is true. This is established convention in both Algol and Lisp, but conversely in arithmetic expressions it would be assumed that all side effects are excited in general. One also feels instinctively uneasy about writing **go to** (**if** *B* **then** *C* **else** *D*) in this form, and indeed PL/I does not appear to provide this locution in any form, though CPL is quite happy with **go to** $B \to C$, *D;*.

13.7 Attributes

As stated earlier, the concept of attributes plays a major part in PL/I and it will be worth while to devote considerable space to seeing how it works out.

Declarations count as statements (but cannot be jumped to and should not be labelled unless for purposes of reference within comment). They take the form

DECLARE ⟨variable list⟩⟨attribute list⟩

where the variable list is either a single identifier or a series of identifiers separated by commas and enclosed in brackets, and the attribute list is a series of words describing the variables being declared. Thus the Algol

integer a, b; **real** x, y; **value** a, b, x;

becomes (keeping the Algol words for the moment)

DECLARE (A, B) INTEGER VALUE;
DECLARE X REAL VALUE;
DECLARE Y REAL NAME;

and one is also allowed to 'factor' the first two thus

DECLARE ((A, B) INTEGER, X REAL) VALUE;

This inversion is a lucidly simplifying stroke for which there is some precedent in Cobol; it transforms the 'properties tree' into the form in which it is usually required, and unifies the syntax with that of statements in general. As well as the type attribute, which we have already discussed, there are others. A variable may be either INTERNAL (=local) or EXTERNAL (= global); this is necessary because a variable used in several modules must be declared in each. Formal parameters are assumed to be INTERNAL, and the earlier proposals also allowed the attribute (by) NAME or (by) VALUE, with the former going by default and no provision for 'simple name'. This has been abandoned in the final specification in favour of determining the attribute at call time (so that it can vary from call to call); an actual parameter which is a simple variable is called by name, one which is a subscripted variable is called by simple name, and one which is an expression (even a single identifier *in brackets*) is called by value. Admittedly this looks more flexible, but it is in fact a retreat, a regrettable victory for a reactionary 'back to Fortran' movement. Variables other than formal parameters can be initialized by the attribute INITIAL (⟨value⟩).

A declaration is not a simple store-raising imperative. The raising of storage — what in Section 5.1 we called the creation of an E-object associated with the L-object which is the name — is dependent on another attribute which may have one of the three values STATIC, AUTOMATIC or CONTROLLED. (The attribute DEFINED, described later, is effectively a fourth value here.) An EXTERNAL variable is STATIC by default; this means that the name is associated with a single location when the various modules are first brought together. An INTERNAL variable is AUTOMATIC by default; this means that the name is associated with a push-down list to which a new location is added each time the procedure is entered and from which one is removed each time it is quitted by RETURN. The declaration INTERNAL STATIC is roughly equivalent to the Algol **own**. A CONTROLLED variable is given an empty push-down list on to which a location is added by the command ALLOCATE, or which is popped up by the command FREE (the imperative being followed by the name of the variable); this permits the control of storage to be kept distinct from the block structure of the programme when need arises.

It is clear from the reports that this aspect of the language is one which received considerable attention. The first report grafted Fortran and Algol together with GLOBAL, LOCAL and OWN. The second combined EXTERNAL/INTERNAL with HELD/TEMP (orary), and introduced ALLOCATE/FREE in an obviously uneasy manner since it referred to a push-down list but said that two ALLO-CATEs in succession implied a FREE between them. (The true push-down list is still required in recursive subroutines.) If the final proposals may be interpreted with the freedom of 'Objective 1' then ALLOCATE L; L = S is the equivalent of Alp's PUSHDOWN (L,S) or IPL-V's 'Function 1' with L as HO; thus (without going into other functions in detail) the introduction of CONTROLLED has provided some of the basic requirements for general list-processing, but the facility of exploring a list, represented by Alp's FIND or IPL-V's J62 would still seem to be lacking in the absence of the dynamic DEFINE elaborated below. The language includes a built-in function ALLOCATE(X) which takes the value **true** if X is sited and **false** if it is not.

A formal parameter is, by its nature, redefined in use by the actual parameter of the call. In the case of a variable which is not a formal parameter, an attribute DEFINED is available which allows the same stored quantity to be referred to in different ways; this feature is a step beyond what Algol or Cobol provided and appears to be a vast improvement on the untidy EQUIVALENCE-COMMON feature of Fortran. One useful application of this may be seen in a declaration such as

DECLARE 1 A DEFINED X, 2 B CHAR(3), 2 C CHAR(4)

Here the initial integers are level-numbers (as in Cobol), and A is said to be declared as a STRUCTURE. Without 'DEFINED X' it declares A to consist of two fields, B of three characters and C of four. As printed it assumes the existence of a previously defined X, possibly a seven-character string on which, by referring to it as A, we can impose the $3+4$ structure. As in Cobol, the first three characters may be referred to as B if this uniquely describes it, otherwise it must be referred to as A.B (where Cobol would have B IN A). In another application of this attribute, identifiers of the form nSUB (meaning the nth subscript, and not permitted except in special contexts such as this) are used in the following way; after, say,

A(M) DEFINED X(I, 2*1SUB+1)

a reference to A(k) will be interpreted as a reference to $X(I, 2k+1)$. Report 1 (which uses a somewhat different notation) quotes

DECLARE X(1000), FLOAT
DEFINE A(M,N), BASE X(1),
ALG((1DIM*(1DIM-1)/2+2DIM)

as being a method of mapping a triangular array on to a vector; Report 2 only permits subscripts *linear* in the nSUB, presumably as a concession to the efficiency of working to be obtained by using index registers for subscripts. 'Objective 1' unquestionably ought to restore the ability to write

DECLARE A(M,N) DEFINED X((1SUB*(1SUB-1))/2+2SUB)

but once again timidity has triumphed over far-sightedness, and 'Objective 1' has been sacrificed to expediency.

The attribute DEFINED means that a variable does not have independent storage. Thus it should be thought of as a fourth value of the allocation attribute, incompatible with any of the other three. Instead of having its own storage, the variable is referred, by means of the defining algorithm, to the storage of some other variable. Allocation of a defined variable therefore comes and goes with that of the variable on which it is defined.

This feature has definite affinities with CPL's initialization by substitution, but is less powerful. So long as it is regarded as there to provide a mapping facility, there is no reason for the defining algorithm to operate other than on the subscripts, but it is only a small step to possibilities like

DECLARE C(P,Q) DEFINED A(1SUB)*B(2SUB)

fuller exploitation of which would soon lead to everything that the CPL technique provides. A rather different extension, replacing the defining algorithm by a dynamic definition, would fill a gap noted earlier. If we could write

DECLARE X DEFINED DYNAMICALLY
:
DEFINE X AS Y
LOOP: FREE X
:

then means would be available for exploring the pushdown list headed by a CONTROLLED Y without losing the head. Neither of the suggestions in this paragraph are a part of PL/I as defined in the final report, however.

13.8 Procedure attributes

When one module calls another, the *name* of the second must be *declared* in the first. It will be declared with PROCEDURE as one of its attributes, and with any others which help in compiling the contexts in which it will be called. The *definition* of the name is the second module itself, which structurally will have the form of an external procedure. (Note that this distinction between declaration and definition does not arise in Algol, where there are no declarations away from the definition, and the definition takes the form of initializing the value of the name to a (constant) piece of programme at the declaration. CPL is similar, at least in all usages which do not involve functions whose values are functions.) The unified syntax of PL/I is nowhere so well exemplified as in the definition of a procedure, which starts with a statement in the form

⟨label⟩ : PROCEDURE ⟨formal par list⟩⟨attributes⟩;

and concludes with a statement *END;* (or, as explained earlier, *END* ⟨label⟩;). The label is mandatory in the opening statement since it is the name of the procedure (or function) for calling purposes. Otherwise the form of this statement is syntactically the same as the DECLARE statement, whereas the comparable construct in former languages has always had a unique syntax. The formal parameter list may be ⟨empty⟩, but if not, it consists of the formal parameters separated by commas and enclosed in brackets in the usual way. (Note, however, that it is not immediately after the procedure name, as it is at a call.) A procedure is invoked as a subroutine by the statement

CALL ⟨procedure label⟩ ⟨actual par list⟩;

and the return is made by a statement *RETURN;*, which is either explicit or else implicit in the final *END;* of the definition. There is no formal distinction between 'routines' and 'functions'; a procedure intended to be used as a function designator must use a statement in the form *RETURN(X)*; to return, where X is an expression whose value is the value required, and there will also be implications on the attribute lists.

Report 2 included another variety of RETURN, namely, the form RETURN TO ⟨name⟩ where the name is a formal parameter of type LABEL. This complemented a rule that a label after a GO TO must belong to the same module, and thus provided a cue to the compiler for recognizing a situation which some Algol compiler writers had found embarrassing. But there was nothing impossible about it, and Report 3 reverts to the Algol technique, dropping RETURN TO and ruling that if the value of the label expression in a GO TO statement is not a label in the same block as the statement itself, then an implied sequence of RETURNs or ENDs will be executed until the programme is on the block-level of the destination-label, before the GO TO is executed.

The attribute concept makes easy the solution of a number of awkward issues, a typical one being the attribute BUILTIN, which allows declaration of a system-defined procedure even though its name has become inaccessible in the ordinary way because it has been used for some other purpose. (By treating the whole set of procedure names as a Cobol structure, this could have been taken further, but this has not been done.)

The attributes in a PROCEDURE *statement* are those which will assist in *compiling the definition*. In Report 2 they are taken from RECURSIVE, a type, EDIT, and SECONDARY, but in Report 3 this has become RECURSIVE, data-attributes (for the result of a *function*) and implementation-dependent options (for external procedures only). SECONDARY was in any case meaningless except on machines with multi-level storage, and EDIT meant that the procedure would be used in the CALL option of a READ or WRITE statement (Section 14.5) — also implementation dependent in significance. The available implementation-dependent options must include MAIN and REENTRANT. (A procedure is REENTRANT whenever, in a multi-programming or parallel-processing situation, it can be simultaneously in use by more than one branch.) In default of a type attribute a function will return a value of the type implicit in the expression attached to the RETURN statement. The attributes appended to the *declaration of a procedure name* are ones which can mostly be determined by inspection of the definition, but which are *useful during independent compilation of the calling procedure*. SETS (⟨list⟩), where the list items are integers (*n* implying *parameter-n*) or names of external variables or * (meaning all external variables), implies that the variables referred to may have their values set (i.e. assigned) by the procedure, and USES (⟨list⟩) similarly indicates

118

what external variables may be read. These assist in optimizing safely. ABNORMAL is a less precise attribute which can be used as a general warner-off; it must also be applied to ordinary variables if, for example, they can become involved in asynchronous processes which might cause their values to change at unpredictable times. INDEFINITE is used if the variable is a formal parameter whose attributes may vary from call to call.

Although a procedure name is syntactically a label, a distinction has to be drawn between procedure names and other labels, and a parameter with a procedure name quality is given the attribute ENTRY, not LABEL. Procedures being briefings and not immediate imperatives, *GO TO X;* where *X* has an ENTRY attribute, if it means anything at all, would seem to mean either 'make sure you have not forgotten what *X* means' or 'go to the point lexicographic-ally following the *END X;*' — since that is the first overt imperative after the label. The word ENTRY is also used as a verb inside a pro-cedure; it does not have the property of bracketing with an *END;*, but its label may be used in a CALL statement to provide alternative entry points, and in this respect it is syntactically and semantically exactly like PROCEDURE. A very interesting development is the GENERIC function. This has numerous entries with inconsistent parameter attributes and (were ABS not built-in) could be used thus:

```
DECLARE ABS GENERIC (ABS1 ENTRY (FIXED), ABS2
    ENTRY (FLOAT REAL), ABS3 ENTRY (COMPLEX));
ABS1: ABS2: PROCEDURE (X); DECLARE Y;
    Y = X; IF Y LT 0 THEN Y = -Y; RETURN(Y);
ABS3: ENTRY (X);
RETURN (SQRT (REAL(X)**2 + IMAG(X)**2));
    END ABS1;
```

When the programme encounters *ABS(Z)* it scans ABS1, ABS2 . . . for an entry where the attributes match those of *Z*. Many of the built-in routines are generic. Note that in the absence of an explicit declaration of attributes for *Y*, *Y = X* declares them 'contextually' to be the same as those of X.

13.9 Other address types

A switch is usually understood to mean a point in a programme at which there is a choice of paths which the control sequence may follow rather more elaborate in nature than a simple conditional transfer of control. Since in principle conditional transfers of control can pro-vide all that is necessary to construct any switch, the term is often reserved for any mechanism which provides a more concise expres-sion of a multi-way option.

The simplest of these is the variable of type **label**. Just as we can write either *x := 2* or *x := y*, so we should be able to write **go to** *P*

119

where, if *P* has been declared in a context '*P:*' it is a constant, but if it has been declared in the context 'label *P;*' then it is a variable whose value will depend on the dynamically most recent assignment statement *P* := *Q* (with *Q* in its turn a constant or a variable whose current value is what is required).

An alternative to this is the fixed label array. If *S* is a label array, then **go to** *S*[*n*] is a method of using the integer *n* to decide between alternative control paths. Two ways of using it may be distinguished, according as the numerical nature of *n* is essential or not. The former will usually betray itself by the occurrence of *n* := *e* where *e* is an expression in which arithmetic is done, as *n* := *n*+*1*. Occasions for the use of such a technique can be constructed. When the only values of *e* are integer constants, one is using *S*[*n*] as a variable *S'* of type label, to which one assigns values chosen from those already in the array. Since Algol makes no provision for free variables of type label, this circumlocution is the only available construction for this technique — as we saw in Section 11.1. Both CPL and PL/I have rectified this omission.

The Algol switch never seemed quite at home in its surroundings. From the syntactic form of its simplest use it appeared to be a cross between a declaration and a peculiar form of assignment statement:

switch S := start, resume, continue;

(all the identifiers on the right being labels). Closer examination shows this particular example to be effectively the declaration of *S* as a **label array** [1:3], with the three members of the array initialized by the assignment, but thereafter immutable because of the absence of provision for free variables of type label and for assignments to this type. In PL/I one can obtain exactly the same effect by writing

DECLARE S (3) LABEL INITIAL (START, RESUME, CONTINUE)

where the '(3)', short for '(1:3)' and occurring immediately after the name, is sufficient to declare *S* a vector. But while this includes the Algol facility, it is actually wider, because the initial values can be changed later, by assignments. Alternatively one may use *S*(*1*), *S*(*2*) and *S*(*3*) as ordinary labels, thus

START: S(1): BEGIN; . . .

This ought, one would think, to give *S*(*1*) the same immutability that *START* has, but apparently this is not so, and we have here an example of the situation described in Section 13.2, with two ways of saying the same thing and no way of saying another. The CPL construction looks different because of the method adopted in CPL for initializing arrays in general — it is

let S = Formarray[**label**, (1:3)][Start, Resume, Continue]

but the effect is identical with that in PL/I. (*Formarray* is a peculiar function of two parameters whose value is another function having

120

a list as parameter. An alternative, *Newarray* [label,(1:3)] sets up the array without initializing it, while **let** S **be vector** (or 1 **array**) declares *S* without siting it or prejudging its size or type.)

But Algol also permits a more complicated construction in a switch — of which

switch S := A, **if** B **then** C **else** D, T[n];

is an example. To this there is no exact equivalent in CPL or PL/I. If one could write

DECLARE S (3) LABEL INITIAL (A, E, F)

and then

DECLARE E DEFINED B*C + (NOT B)*D
DECLARE F DEFINED T(N)

one would have the right effect, but this lies outside the permitted use of DEFINE, as well as raising once again the question of 'conditional label expressions'. CPL would find something of this sort less difficult to write — for example,

let S = Formarray [label,(1:3)][A,E,F] **where** E = B → C, D, etc. The problem which the Algol construction raises acutely is that it requires us to initialize some components of the array by value and others by name!

Incidentally, with *S* defined as above, **go to** S[2] would be interpreted correctly if the second item in *S* were replaced by a new label *E*, and a new statement

E : **go to if** B **then** C **else** D

were added somewhere in the programme. But this does not cover everything; there is one context in which storage of an address as the value of an E-object seems unavoidable (except that the fixed-array trick is always available). This is when S[2] occurs as a parameter in a routine and is called by value; in this context the choice between C and D depends on the value of B at the moment of entry to the routine and not on its value when **go to** S[2] is executed.

13.10 Loop facilities

In Algol, **begin** . . . **end** surrounds a block if declarations follow the **begin**, but a compound statement if they do not. In PL/I a block is surrounded by BEGIN; . . . END; and a 'group' by DO; . . . END;. The DO; may be expanded in one of two ways

DO WHILE ⟨logical expression⟩;
DO ⟨variable⟩ = ⟨iteration list⟩;

the second of these providing a similar facility to the Algol for-statement, and the former something which was unaccountably absent from the Algol for-repertoire. Each item in the iteration list is of the form

⟨expressn⟩ BY ⟨expressn⟩ TO ⟨expressn⟩ WHILE ⟨expressn⟩ in which 'while true' or 'by 1' may be omitted, BY and TO may be interchanged, TO ⟨expression⟩ may be omitted, or the first expression may stand alone or with only the while-clause. The controlled variable is called by simple name, the while-expression by name and the other expressions by value. Commas separate the items.

In CPL, iteration without a controlled variable is also provided for by **while** ⟨boolean⟩ **do** ⟨command⟩, and ⟨command⟩ **repeat while** ⟨boolean⟩; these cause zero and (at least) one execution, respectively, of the command if entered with the boolean initially **false**. (Or **true** if **until** replaces **while**.) The controlled variable type has a luxurious variety of syntactic variations all representing the same semantics apart from explicit or implicit ($=1$) representation of the increment; in the following, the first line is a simple list for successive use and the other lines are all step-until elements (all 'identifiers' represent *expressions*):

    for v = E1, E2, E3, E4,
        F1 **to** F2,
        G1, G2, ..., G3,
        step H1, H2, H3 || H2 is the increment
        I1 **step** I2 **to** I3

But 'J1 **while** B' appears to have been omitted; in isolation it is equivalent to '**while** B **do** § $v :=$ J1; ... §' but this does not provide for it as a member of a longer list. None of these is identical to the Algol 'E1 **step** E2 **until** E3' because the semantics is not the same as in Algol, and confusion might arise. In effect the controlled variable is treated as a parameter of the procedure Y of the expansion in Section 11.3, and the whole expansion as an outer procedure of which the E's are parameters *all these parameters* being called by *value*. Suppose that v has the value 5. Then whereas Algol

    for v := 1 **step** v **until** 12 **do begin** X; v := v+1 **end**

leads to doing X with $v = 1, 4, 10$ and exits with v undefined, the CPL

    for v = **step** 1, v, 12 **do** § X; v := v+1 §

leads to doing X with $v = 1, 6, 11$ and on exit v is still 5. By writing '**for ext** v = ... ' one can call the controlled variable by (simple) name — but this will not affect the increment. Thus the CPL semantics are nearer to those of PL/I but not quite identical with them. Since (a) simple cases are equivalent, and (b) the provision of this facility is a convenience and not a necessity (because the loop can always be written out in full), there is little point in embarking on a detailed appreciation; perhaps the main virtue of the CPL interpretation is that v need not be declared elsewhere *at all*. There is also something to be said for the argument that when something is

122

offered as a convenience, and therefore made attractive, it should also be made convenient to the machine, and therefore efficient.

13.11 Unique features

The foregoing sections by no means exhaust the comparisons which could be made — for example, a useful study could be made of the increasing number of built-in functions which newer languages provide, and the relation between current practice and real needs in this respect. But this would be a very lengthy study, and we may conveniently conclude the present chapter by mentioning certain features possessed uniquely by one or other of these two languages as at present defined.

We mentioned in Section 9.5 that Cobol has found the need to introduce AT END and ON SIZE ERROR as a conditional statement alternative to an IF statement. PL/I has developed this not only for traps but to handle the requirements of parallel processing. Anticipation of traps is provided for by the ON statement — ON⟨emergency name⟩⟨emergency action⟩, which can provide general anticipation by standing in its own right, or provide specific anticipation at a particular point in a programme by being appended to any other statement (as in Cobol). Names are provided for the commoner emergencies, and systems with special ones will provide names for them. A programmer can invent his own traps giving them his own names, and cause them to occur by the statement SIGNAL ⟨name⟩. There is also a variant of the CALL statement which takes the form

CALL ⟨proc name⟩(⟨arg list⟩), COMPLETE(⟨log variable⟩)

(Syntactically very similar to an attribute, an addition to an executive statement such as this is called an 'option'.) The CALL then sets the logical variable to 'false' and the RETURN sets it to 'true', and the calling and called procedures may be executed in parallel. This is complemented by a statement in the calling procedure WAIT(⟨list⟩), with an option WAIT(⟨list⟩), ANY(⟨expression⟩), where the list is of logical variables and the expression is numerical; this holds up the calling procedure until all the logical variables are 'true' or until the number which are 'true' exceeds the value of the expression. For dealing with peripherals the logical variables may be hardware states with system-defined names. CPL does not, in its present form, make any provision for parallel processing.

A 'structure' is an immutable list-structure whose parts are all named, and need not be homogeneous in type as those of an array must be. Well-established through the Cobol tradition, it is provided for at the heart of PL/I by the incorporation of level numbers into the normal process of declaration. CPL would appear to relegate it to a very subsidiary position; in in/output it is recognized that a file may be structured in this way, but it is ignored in the more central language. On the other hand, PL/I does not seem to have made any adequate provision for flexible list-structures, whereas CPL has a type **list** with all the necessary functions (and, incidentally, 'head' and 'tail' for 'car' and 'cdr') which list processing languages have shown to be required. A feature of CPL is the way it has incorporated lists into other areas of programming, particularly in the 'simultaneous assignment' such as

$$x, y := x+1, y+1$$

In such a statement all the right-hand side expressions are evaluated before any assignments are made. Thus $x,y := y,x$ is a genuine interchange of values.

A unique feature of PL/I which probably derives from various local extensions to Fortran is the symbol '%'. Standing at the beginning of a line, it indicates that the statement concerned is to be obeyed, not compiled, at compile time. Its primary purpose is to provide a 'macro' facility within the language, and thus to make the language open-ended (i.e. able to define new idioms for itself). This is a development which will be watched with interest. [See also Section 15.2.4.]

CPL may well be the only language which permits statements to occur within expressions, although this is only the extension of the idea of open and closed subroutines to functions. One can write statements like

$$x := a + \textbf{result of } \S \ldots \S$$

The $\S \ldots \S$ must contain within it a statement **result is** . . . , which is the exit cue. This facility is rather cramped by the 'no side effects' dogma, otherwise one could see it being of use diagnostically — at a point of suspected trouble one could replace x in an expression by **result of** $\S$ print(x); **result** $= x \S$ and thus keep track of what was happening!

Finally, a matter in respect of which even CPL seems to be taking a very wary attitude — the function-generating function. If we define

$$F = \lambda(a,b,c)[\lambda(x).(a+bx+cx^2)]$$

and then make the assignment $G := F(1,2,1)$, we have defined G as the function $G(x) = (1+x)^2$. The Landin approach regards such an action as all in the day's work. But it has its new problems. If G is declared in an outer block (without any initial assignment of value), and the assignment is made in an inner block using local variables as parameters, then the assignment must remain valid throughout the outer block. (Compare

begin integer a; **begin integer** b; b := 1; a := b **end**; print(a) **end**

which gives no trouble at all.) CPL is the first language to arrive at the point where this is a possibility to be considered, and this is another development to watch.

14
INPUT AND OUTPUT

Input and output routines represent an interface between languages — between the language in which the programming is written and that in which the data is written. It is therefore quite wrong to require each language to have a fully developed input-output system before it can be recognized; what is required is a supralinguistic standard so set out that it is possible for languages to conform to it without violating their own internal conventions. Of course, such a standard will make certain minimum demands on all languages, and if existing languages fail to meet these demands we can do no more than to ensure that we understand why. But for the future, what we suggest is by no means an impossible objective.

We are not concerned with the detailed functioning of input and output organs, but only with the relations we wish to set up between, on the one hand, certain sets of L- and E-objects in the computer and their values, and, on the other, certain graphic symbols occurring in a certain layout on a printed page. What passes across the interface must, therefore, be a string of characters combining 'graphic' and 'layout' information. But at a language level which transcends machine dependence, the layout part of this string must be descriptive of the layout achieved and not of how any specific equipment achieves it. A crucial example here is the concept of pre-set 'tabs'. On a typewriter these are a specific mechanical feature, preset by one manipulation of the keys and called by another, while on a teleprinter there is no equivalent, and the effect must be simulated by programming. We, however, must simply take note (a) of the existence of 'tab' as a character in the I.S.O. set, and (b) that it has a semantic which makes it a very useful high-level feature for layout description in any language — this and no more.

Input and output routines have much in common while differing in two fundamental respects. In the first place, output routines are in control of what happens, while input routines must, within reason, accept what they are given. In particular, output routines create a layout; input routines find one and, apart from using what they find for interpretive purposes, throw it away. Secondly, literals can be copied to output, but in pure procedures input material can only be assigned to a variable (of type *string* if we wish). For both reasons it is

125

usual to make output the prime consideration, and then to adapt the conventions decided upon into a corresponding input system.

14.1 Early languages

The problems which have to be overcome in any completely adequate output scheme fall into a number of categories which interweave in a most perplexing manner:

1. There are three levels of format control
   (a) Overall matters such as page size (margins both at the sides and top and bottom of pages, etc) and inclusion or exclusion of line numbers, page headings, etc,
   (b) Inter-item formats — broadly speaking, deciding where on the page the next item begins, and
   (c) Intra-item formats, concerning the way in which the value of a given variable is reproduced graphically quite apart from its position on the page.
2. All output is, in the last resort, output of character strings, at any rate while we remain within the definitions of Section 1.2. A well-defined set of transfer functions from all other types to this one is therefore a first requisite — but these must be flexible (e.g. it must be possible to output to a lesser precision than is used for the computation).
3. But, for the automation of office work, a backing store is equivalent in many ways to hard copy (e.g. it can constitute the archives). To put it mildly, this qualifies conclusions based on (1) and (2).
4. There are two respects in which the distinction between 'command' and 'briefing' appears once more:
   (a) Provision must be made for 'presetting' (i.e. preparative) commands which produce no immediate output but set a condition which will determine how subsequent output commands will be interpreted. These may be hardware or software interpreted, as with 'tab-setting' on typewriter or teleprinter.
   (b) It is very inconvenient if a control character such as carriage-return cannot be referred to in the programming language without exciting the corresponding effect, so that 'neutralized equivalents' of these characters are required.
5. The environment division of Cobol brings to our notice a number of issues which are ignored by other languages. One important one is the designation of output organs in a programme by 'logical' references which must somehow be related at run-time to actual hardware devices. It will be convenient to use the phrase 'environment control' to cover these requirements, however met.

Historically, it must be remembered that Autocodes were intended in the first instance for mathematical work. In these cases intelligibility and ease of reading are important in the output, but unless facsimiles

126

are to be included in a report, elegance, including all *paging*, is un-necessary. Moreover, Autocodes were most often intended for a restricted group of machines and therefore for a restricted variety of output systems. Usually Autocodes contain a NEWLINE *order* and are opaque to the corresponding character in the output, which serves as a statement terminator. A CAPTION *order* provides for output of a whole line as a literal. All other output is confined to the current line, which is built up by programming from three types of output— short literals, groups of spaces, and numbers in a specifiable format (e.g. '5 sig.fig., 2 integral'). The technique of format specification is sometimes *print*(x, 5, 2), and sometimes *print*(x,'dd.ddd'). With these facilities there is no difficulty in organising a layout such as

TRIALS SIMULATION RESULTS
RUN NO.6   R = 500 YARDS;   T2 = 0.05 SECS.

T	X	Y
000.0	00000	00000
000.1	00216	00050
000.2	00405	00098

SIMULATION STOPPED BECAUSE OF EMERGENCY NO.12

but there is a lack of all higher-level facilities, including any ability to lay down a format in advance.

Fortran introduced the explicit format statement designed to specify a format which could later be called upon. In Basic Fortran a format description, or $\langle FD \rangle$, is one of the following,

nX meaning n blanks (spaces)
$nH\langle string \rangle$ literal (n must be the number of characters in the string)
rIw r w-character integers
$rFw.d$ r real numbers of w characters, d digits after the point, and no exponent part.
$rEw.d$ the same but including an exponent part

Whenever $r = 1$ it may be omitted. To these full Fortran adds rLw for logical ($w - 1$ blanks, then T or F), rAw for r w-character fields to be filled from the list (see below), and certain further varieties of real. The full syntax of a format statement (or$\langle FS \rangle$) is

$\langle FS \rangle ::= \langle label \rangle FORMAT(\$0\{/\}\$0\langle spec\ gp \rangle\$0\{/\})$
$\langle spec\ gp \rangle ::= \uparrow 1\langle integer \rangle(\langle spec\ gp\ \rangle)|\langle FD \rangle\$0\{\langle sepr \rangle\langle FD \rangle\}$
$\langle sepr \rangle ::= ,|\ \$1\{/\}$

i.e. the argument of FORMAT is a series of $\langle FD \rangle$ separated by com-mas or slashes and with provision for abbreviating repetitions by use of coefficients. The format statement is, of course, a monstrosity of the same sort as the Algol switch, a declaration with initialization of a type of variable to which assignments cannot otherwise be made — in this case a string variable. Input/output statements take the form

$$\{READ|WRITE\}(\langle unit\rangle\uparrow 1\{,\langle format\ label\rangle\})\uparrow 1\langle list\rangle$$

where $\langle unit\rangle$ is an integer specifying (by a correspondence established through an environment control) the input/output organ to be used, and the list specifies the variables (or states the literals) whose values are to be transferred. The latter may take forms like

$$'P = ',\ P,\ (R(S),\ S = 0,\ 1,\ N)$$

including recursive use of the loop specification. Of the two simplest forms

$$READ(\langle unit\rangle)\qquad WRITE(\langle unit\rangle)$$

the latter is meaningless, but the former can occur as a function designator. The list will be empty if the format is entirely literal, and the format can go by default when it contains no literals. It is assumed that input does, or output will, consist of *records* composed of *fields*, and in the formats, commas separate fields and slashes separate records. Elaborate rules provide interpretations, wherever possible, in cases of mismatch; broadly speaking (1) an excess of format information is skipped, (2) a deficit of format information is made up by repetition of the last item used, and (3) a slash in a format when there are still fields in the current record will cause these to be skipped. (Note that Algol treats (2) by falling back on standard format, and PL/I by repetition of the *whole* format.) READ is a procedure with side effects in that it leaves input looking at the start of the *next* record after the one just read. There are three auxiliary procedures, BACKSPACE($\langle unit\rangle$), which steps input back to the beginning of the currently just read *record*, ENDFILE($\langle unit\rangle$) which writes an end of file mark, and REWIND($\langle unit\rangle$) which steps input right back to the beginning of the *file*.

Cobol assumes the existence of buffer areas containing the last-read or next-to-be-written record of each file, and of associated routines compiled in accordance with the information in the Environment and Data divisions. READ and WRITE orders are thus very simple, no formatting being involved. Every variable has its picture and format changes are effected by the MOVE verb. (The fact that arithmetic may actually be done in binary is not mentioned in polite society except through the euphemism USAGE IS COMPUTATIONAL.) Thus the contribution of Cobol may be said to be the development of the picture — with Fortran suggesting that '6A' may be preferable to either 'PICTURE IS AAAAAA' or 'SIZE IS 6 ALPHABETIC' — and the concept of environment control.

14.2 Algol and Algol/IFIP

Fortran had the advantage of being developed for the machines of a particular company; Algol essayed independence of machine characteristics over a much wider range, and therefore assumed that it was

128

almost inevitable that in/out procedures would have to be written in machine code. For a long time it refused to provide even specifications for such procedures, but those holding this position were politically out-manoeuvred when I.S.O. made provision of explicit in/output a prerequisite for recognition of a language. Two sets of proposals were then issued, at such different levels as not to be rivals. An IFIP committee (1964) issued a set of seven 'primitives', with the aid of which anything more complicated could be built up in true Algol, and an ACM committee (Knuth, 1964) issued a set of proposals which expanded the Fortran system using all the virtuosity of Algol. The latter has been revised to include the former.

Prior to this development, each implementation produced its own solution, usually in terms of globally defined procedures. The Elliott implementers preferred **print** *x,y;* to *print(x,y)*, and by thus introducing a new statement type to the syntax they avoided breaking other rules normally binding on procedure statements — though whether these rules have to be binding on procedures written in machine code has never really been cleared up. The crucial difficulties arise from two rules in particular. (a) A procedure with an Algol body has to be declared with a fixed number of parameters (and no type **list** exists to ease this); (b) When the type of a parameter is specified (and this is compulsory in some implementations) it cannot be varied from call to call, so that separate procedures are required for numerical and string outputs. This leaves a choice between a set of procedures at the Autocode level, or the assumption that one or both of the rules mentioned are not binding on procedures whose bodies are in machine code. Both options have been selected at various times.

Because Algol is so essentially a language for numerical work, the first two of the IFIP primitives are *insymbol* and *outsymbol*, both with three parameters. These are (1) an integer *channel* the meaning of which is established by environment control, (2) a string whose characters are implicitly mapped on to the integers 1, 2 . . . , and (3) a second integer variable whose value, by virtue of the mapping, is or becomes the value of the single character written or read. Algol symbols not in the string will map on to zero and non-Algol symbols acquire an implementation-dependent association with a negative number. The third primitive is the integer procedure *length*(⟨string or string variable⟩), whose value is the number of characters in its parameter. (There are no free string variables in Algol, but bound string variables can occur.) The remaining four of the seven procedures are *inreal*, *outreal*, *inarray* and *outarray*, each with two parameters, a *channel* and a *source* or *destination* of appropriate type. These are not primitive in the same sense, as they can be written in terms of the first three with one exception — that for the last two another primitive would be required giving explicit access to information which must exist about the shape of an array whose name only is available as a parameter. (Indeed, an '*ininteger*' is so written in the report to show how it can be done.)

The IFIP procedures permit the accurate definition, in Algol, of the procedures actually required or available for in/output in a given context; it may be doubted whether they are likely to be used practically. Who, for example, would willingly employ

```
procedure outstring(channel, string); value channel;
   begin integer i;
   for i := 1 step 1 until length(string) do
       outsymbol (channel, string, i) end;
outstring (1, 'GRAND TOTAL = ');
```

when a procedure body in machine code for *outstring* would short-circuit most of the machinery involved? Their theoretical interest is more difficult to assess; they arise out of certain deficiencies of Algol, but is, in fact, a character-to-integer mapping procedure not likely to be required sooner or later even in a language which is not so numerically bound as Algol?

14.3 Algol/ACM

The wider ACM proposals contain many features of interest. In the first place they demand a technique which has always been available but little recognized, known as the *list procedure*. It depends only on the ability to write a function or procedure name as an actual parameter, and is therefore available in Fortran (though not in Basic Fortran). Where the rule requiring a fixed number of parameters would be broken by

A1:   print(a, b);   print(x, y, z);
the list procedure technique attacks this situation thus:
```
procedure list1(X); procedure X;
   begin X(a); X(b) end;
procedure list2(X); procedure X;
   begin X(x); X(y); X(z) end;
   :
   :
```
A2:   list1(print);   list2(print);

The line labelled *A2* is legal and identical in effect with the more obvious but illegal sequence *A1*. Moreover there is nothing special about the list procedure, which can be written to include use of any facility normally available — for example

```
procedure list3(X, Q); procedure X; boolean Q;
   begin integer i; if Q then
   for i := 1 step 1 until n do X(V[i]) end;
```

It can also include format revising statements. Note that although

130

this device relaxes a number of constraints, it does nothing to permit flexibility of type in implementations where this is lacking.

Actual output calls may be made at two levels of sophistication. The more general is in the form

outlist(channel, layout, list)

formally identical with the Fortran scheme except that as both *layout* and *list* are procedure names, and not a statement label and an actual list, both occur as parameters. The effect of such a call is first to standardize the situation and then to call *layout*, which makes any modifications to the standard situation which may be desired. The elements of this situation include setting of margins and nomination of emergency procedures for line or page overflow as well as format information of a more conventional kind. Then, briefly, *list* is called with a single-item output routine as argument. The full story is a complicated one owing to the necessity to check for line or page over-flow, possibly calling an emergency procedure which alters formats or margins, before actually activating the item-output routine. These checking procedures are procedures declared within *outlist* and called both openly within it and also from the item-output routine when this is called from within the list-procedure.

The less sophisticated output is a higher level facility consisting of a series of routines defined for $n = 0, 1, \ldots 9$ in terms of *outlist* thus

```
procedure outputn(channel, formatstring, e₁, . . . eₙ);
  begin procedure A; format(formatstring);
    procedure B(P); begin P(e₁); . . . P(eₙ) end;
  outlist (channel, A, B) end
```

As will have been observed in the above definition, a format is set by a system-defined procedure *format* which takes a string as parameter. Innocent of all actual illegality, this procedure makes an assignment to a *hidden* variable of type string. The information which can be conveyed by the format string goes beyond anything that either Fortran or Cobol permit. The first level deep in quotes is all in a Cobol-picture-like code, and literals go a second layer deep. The full syntax is too long to reproduce here but the following summary shows how the code level is interpreted.

$\langle R \rangle ::= \langle integer \rangle | X$ numerals form unsigned integers used as replicating co-efficients. X is a dynamically evaluated replicator described later

$\langle A \rangle ::= \uparrow 1 \langle R \rangle \{/| \uparrow | J\}$ /, $\uparrow$, J are newline, newpage and tab symbols — alignment marks — used alone or with a replicator

131

⟨fs⟩ ::= '⟨F1⟩'| " a format string is an Algol string and may be empty (indicating an implementation defined standard format).
N also denotes this standard format applied to single items.

⟨F1⟩ ::= ⟨F2⟩|⟨F1⟩,⟨F2⟩ Commas separate items (⟨F3⟩) or replicated item groups

⟨F2⟩ ::= ⟨F3⟩|⟨R⟩(⟨F1⟩)|(⟨F1⟩) Brackets are used for nested replication. The third alternative denotes replication *ad inf* — as might be needed if the list contains a for-list.

⟨F3⟩ ::= ⟨F4⟩|⟨A⟩|⟨F3⟩⟨A⟩ An ⟨F3⟩ is one of six type-formats possibly associated with alignment marks on one or both sides.

⟨F4⟩: := ⟨A⟩⟨F4⟩|one of . . .

title format, using B and quote-marks Consisting only of blanks and material deeper in quotes — known as insertions.

nonformat, using I, L, R (system dependent — maybe each I L or R is picture for one octal digit) Next item on list, converted if necessary to integer, boolean or real type, then output in *internal* machine representation.

boolean format using P or F **false** is '0' on P, 'F' on F, or 'FALSE' on 5F; **true** is '1'. 'T', or 'TRUE '.

numerical format using D, T, Z, +, −, $_{10}$, V, dec.pt. Almost identical with the Cobol picture code; T denotes truncation *without* round-off

string format using S and alpha format using A for strings externally, held internally as strings and integers respectively (the latter is implementation dependent).

Two points in this summary need amplification. (1) The X replicator. It would have been possible to introduce special brackets into format strings with the meaning that, for example, '/[k]B' should imply a new line followed by as many spaces as the current value of the integer variable *k*. This would certainly have led to considerable compilation difficulties, unless one could be certain of always recognizing when a string is a format string. It has been preferred to make such integer expressions into parameters outside the string, and this has meant supplementing *format* with the series *format n* and using them thus: the call

format 1('/XB', k)

creates the effect we want. More generally, the string of a *format n*

132

contains n X's which are replaced at call time by the current values of the remaining parameters in order. (2) The detailed syntax of the type formats allows for 'insertions' almost anywhere; thus it is legal to write

output1(1, 'ZZD'‿dollars‿'DDB'cents", 2↑10)

and the result would be

‿10‿dollars‿24‿cents

No other major language as yet provides this facility.

There are routines similar to *format* for defining margin settings, nominating 'on overflow' procedures, and so on. It is understood that calls of these procedures are only effective when made from within *outlist* (or *inlist*) — i.e. when they have been written by the programmer within a procedure which is elsewhere made a parameter of *outlist*. By the general rules of 'scope' in Algol, if a call of a procedure within a block (or procedure declaration) is valid and the procedure is not declared at the head of that block, then a similar call is valid in the encompassing block. However, calls of these procedures in 'open programme' would produce no effect that could be detected except by output, and would be overridden at the next output call.

It is also necessary to be on guard against easy association of equivalence between idioms in different languages. Thus it is true that a call *nodata(A)* of the system defined **procedure** *nodata (L);* **label** *L; . . . ;*, is the Algol equivalent of the Cobol AT END GO TO A, in the sense that it is an alternative idiom more congenial to Algol syntax in general and with the same elementary semantics. But there are at least eight alternative variations of how L may be treated in complex situations. In the first place, is there *one* hidden L, or *one per file* (in Algol, *per channel*)? And alongside this, is the statement:

(a) an irredeemable initialization,

(b) a value for that (lexicographic) call only,

(c) an assignment to a label-type variable,

or (d) a putting of the value on a pushdown list, popped up on leaving the routine from which the statement was made?

Cobol manages both (a) and (b) according to context. The Algol proposal is either (c) or (d). On which, depends the effect of, for example, calling *outlist* in the middle of a layout or list procedure.

14.4 Input/output in PL/I

PL/I has very elaborate arrangements for in/output, and it is unlikely that any brief account could avoid being misleading under some circumstances or other. Subject to this warning, we may say that it is based upon the following

⟨i/o⟩ ::= {READ| WRITE}⟨xxx⟩⟨data specification⟩⟨option list⟩;
⟨xxx⟩ ::= FILE(⟨name⟩),| STRING(⟨name⟩),|⟨empty⟩

The string alternative is used for all internal transfers which call for editing to be done, and the empty alternative implies use of a standard (input or output) file. With the string alternative the option list must be empty. In other cases, one record is processed, mismatches being dealt with much as in Fortran unless the option list includes one of (a)

$$\text{CROSS} \uparrow 1 \{(\langle\text{integer exp} = n\rangle)\}\uparrow 1\{\text{HOLD}\}$$

in which case $n - 1$ record boundaries may be crossed and if HOLD is present there is no skip to the beginning of a new record, and (b) SEGMENT($\langle$character exp$\rangle$), which implies both CROSS and HOLD and uses the character expression as an intersegment marker (one segment being read or written). Other options permit the file to be used sequentially or searched on a key, permit input data to be simultaneously written on the standard output file, allow recognition of trailing zero suppression in fractions, and allow the source of a WRITE statement to be, not working space, but the buffer of a named input file.

The data description consists of a list of variables (including non-scalars) and associated formats. The latter are those required or expected in the file, and if they differ from the declared attributes of the variables some editing will be involved. There are four varieties of data description, corresponding to four modes of data transmission, examples of each are

List-directed: WRITE LIST (A*B,(M(I) I = 1 TO 5));
Data-directed: WRITE DATA (M);
Format-directed: WRITE ('RESULT IS ', X) (A, F(5,2));
Procedure-directed: WRITE $\langle$as above$\rangle$, CALL P;

In each of these examples the standard output file is used and the option list is empty. In *list-directed* transmission the items must be scalar; output format is controlled by the attributes of the scalars and a 'tab' separator, while input format is that of constants in the language (except, oddly, that two numbers of which the second is signed and *not* separated from the first by a blank is a complex number and this does not apply *within* the language). It is permitted, in a second bracket after the list, to nominate a different item separator. In *data-directed output* non-scalar names are permitted; if M is a matrix then WRITE DATA (M) is equivalent to

$$\text{WRITE DATA (((M(I,J) J = JMIN TO JMAX) I =} \\ \text{IMIN TO IMAX))}$$

(i.e. the later subscripts vary more rapidly). Each scalar item is output in the form '$\langle$name$\rangle = \langle$value$\rangle$'. On *input* this form is expected and the list can be used as a check or omitted, but names which may turn up without warning like this must be given a SYMBOL attribute on declaration so that the translator knows that it must compile a dictionary for use at run time. Not all the elements in the list need

134

be found in the input at one read, nor need the order in which they occur agree with the list.

In *format-directed* transmission the format in the external medium is explicitly provided according to a code in which:

F refers to fixed-point layout
E floating-point layout
C complex layout
P format defined by picture
A string length
R remote format (with the label of a FORMAT statement as parameter)
IF, etc, the internal layout as declared for a fixed-point (etc) number.

Interspersed between these item-formats may be positioning formats SPACE, SKIP, GROUP, TAB (each with an optional parameter which is an integer replicator) or POSITION(⟨format list⟩) which repositions the external medium by going to the beginning of the record and recapping (without doing anything) the specified format. These positioning format-items may also be used as statements.

More complicated cases are dealt with by the *procedure-directed* option. A statement WRITE . . . , CALL X; is equivalent to WRITE . . . ; CALL X; with this exception, that the name of the file which is the object of the WRITE is placed on a pushdown list known as the current-file (normally empty), and the file at the top of this list can be referenced by PUT (for WRITE) and GET (for READ). On the return from X the list is popped-up. As an example, the situation described in Section 9.4, where one does not know which type of record is coming up next, can be dealt with in the following way (among others)

    READ FILE (COSTS FILE), (ITEM)(A(1)), CROSS(1) HOLD,
        CALL J;
        :
        :

J: PROCEDURE;
    IF ITEM = 'W' THEN DO; GET(WAGE_DETAIL)(A(26));
    . . . END; ELSE IF ITEM = 'P' THEN DO; GET(PURCH_
    DETAIL)(A(22); . . . END;
    ELSE SIGNAL BADCARD;
    END J;

There are no restrictions on the way calls of this sort may be nested.

Files must be OPENed and CLOSEd, and these verbs have options which deal with file-identification labels, and, in the case of OPEN, with much of the information which Cobol puts in the environment division, one result of which is to remove the inflexibility of the Cobol

K

arrangements and make them alterable during the course of a run. FETCH and DELETE are used to bring in library programmes (to be subsequently invoked by a CALL statement) and to free the storage again when the process is finished with. These are interesting in that it is legal to write

FETCH('PROG' || N)

which, since || is the concatenation operator, will have the effect of converting the value of N to a string and concatenating it with 'PROG', and thus calling a routine with the name 'PROGn' (n an integer). One then uses the same trick in the parameter of CALL. But for some reason, the report makes it sound as if one is not allowed to do this with one's own routine names — a strange lapse from 'objective 1' since to allow the SYMBOL attribute to a PROCEDURE statement would seem to cover any difficulties. (Of course, one would then logically have to allow the same to *any* label, and this would raise more problems.) Another form of output is

DISPLAY(⟨string exp⟩)↑1 REPLY(⟨string variable⟩)

which displays the expression on the monitor typewriter and, if the REPLY is included, suspends the programme until the message is acknowledged with contents for the variable. This eliminates need for the ACCEPT verb of some languages. There are also separate PAGE and LAYOUT statements for presetting page-size, -heading, etc, and margins respectively.

SAVE and RESTORE statements, each with an item-list and optionally an integer-expression tag, write and read respectively on a 'dump file'. For each distinct variable this provides effectively one push-down list (untagged SAVEs and RESTOREs) and an unlimited number of single, numbered, reserve stores. The items must be scalars or *complete* arrays or structures. These are not strictly in/out statements unless these are held to include *all* transmission to and from *files* of any description. So far as list-processing is concerned, once again (as with CONTROLLED) a pushdown list is not an adequate provision, unless means are also available to explore its depths non-destructively.

14.5 Input/output in CPL

In arranging that initially London and Cambridge are each issuing their own in/output manual, CPL would appear to subscribe to the Algol assumption that in/output must be allowed to be installation dependent. The availability of **list** and **general** as types bypasses most of the linguistic problems encountered in other languages, leaving only the layout problems which all languages have to solve. In only two respects does CPL show an individuality which calls for comment. (1) On account of the 'no side-effects' rule, it is necessary to have

(a) a *procedure* with parameter x which assigns to x the *next* value on the tape, and holds a record of it, and

(b) a *function* whose value is the *currently recorded* input value and which does not have the side effect of advancing the tape.

(2) As explained in Section 13.5, the method used for neutralizing control characters is not the usual one of a 'format code', but is the nomination of one character to the office of 'escape symbol'.

14.6 Conclusions

This is not the place to try to set up a standard of the sort which, in the introduction to this chapter, we declared to be desirable, but it is possible to set out certain conclusions on which a consensus of opinion seems already to have been reached. It may be doubted whether any new language will arise which does not embody the concept of calling a procedure with parameters, whatever notation it may use for this, and therefore it is unlikely that it will impose any constraint on any future language if a standard is defined in terms of this concept. Granting this, it seems to be agreed that it is desirable to work in terms of two main procedures, one for input and one for output, each of which has three parameters. The first of these is either a file name or an integer denoting the channel. In either case an association with actual hardware must be set up by environment control, and as a specification for environment control will probably have to be part of the proposed standard, conflicting traditions will probably be reconciled in the process of producing this specification.

The second and third parameters define the format and enumerate the constants and variables concerned in the process. (Constants must be in the list if call dependent, but may be in the format if call independent.) Which of these is second and which third is a trivial decision on which somebody will have to give way. To accept the standard a language will have to be able to handle a list, but may do it in its own way, e.g.

naturally, as (in different ways) in CPL and PL/I

by list-procedures as in Algol (and possibly Fortran)

by using structure-names, array-names, or names of pushdown lists

by not imposing any rule which enforces a fixed number of parameters. (This favours format as second parameter and *the rest* as list.)

The format parameter must make provision for three things — control items, literal strings, and translation of variable values from internal to external representation. For this some sort of code is essential; if it takes the form of a string, then it is necessary that the language can handle strings at least to the extent of accepting such a string, but once this has been accepted, a code of the proposed Algol

137

type has one advantage too great to be thrown away — the internal details of the code are completely insulated from the syntax of the language and can conform to an external standard independently of it. Thus the Algol type of format will be far easier to fit into any new language than one like the PL/I type. The advantages of PL/I lie, not in its format arrangements, which are clumsy in comparison, but in its options, and an acceptable in/out standard will have to permit incorporation of these — particularly the data-controlled option. In a language without options but with format procedures, a system procedure could effect this. It may be hazarded, however, that options will prove popular — suppose one could write, in Algol,

$$C := A \times B, \text{termbyterm}; \quad D := A \times B, \text{matrix};$$

what an advantage it would be! But even PL/I has not got round to this yet.

A note added during reprinting: Certain revisions have been made in PL/I since publication of the reports on which this and the previous chapter were based, and some of the statements are in consequence no longer true. This applies particularly to the use of '=' in assignment statements and the boolean equality relations, and to the precedence of **.

15

MISCELLANEOUS TOPICS

The foregoing chapters have, as it were, explored the main line of programming languages, in which three sources — machine languages, mathematical formalism, and the requirements of business data-processing — have developed until they have overlapped, while concurrently the mathematical theory of language has become available to explain, co-ordinate, codify and control much of what was in the first place empirical in their practice. But there have also been developments which, for one reason or another, have been out of the main stream, yet deserve mention.

15.1 Special purpose languages

A large number of languages of considerable variety have been produced for special purposes. Because every language must have a character set and an unambiguous, decidable grammar, and probably has at least a limited requirement for handling strings and numbers (English and Arithmetic, if you like), individual consideration of any of these languages is apt to involve much recapitulation of ground already covered, and any features of real interest, when arrived at, turn out to belong to the special nature of the intended application. Nevertheless, they cannot altogether be ignored.

Comit (Yngve, 1961) and Snobol (Farber *et al*, 1964) are 'string processing' languages. Thus they may be thought of as procedure type equivalents to the function language Macro-generator. Since all lists can, by the use of brackets, be represented as strings, they might be regarded as a subset of list-processing languages, but compared with those mentioned in Section 12 they are more restricted, and consequently they are more efficient within their chosen fields, less efficient outside them. A recent candidate for inclusion in this group is 'Axle, An axiomatic language for string transformation' (Cohen and Wegstein, 1965), but since a programme in Axle appears to consist of two tables (an assertion table and an imperative table), one is led to wonder whether the word 'language' is a useful one in this case, even if it can be justified technically by provision of vocabulary and grammar.

Two further groups, somewhat overlapping, are composed of (1) languages with special features for statistical processes and (2) simulation languages. The overlap arises when stochastic variables are involved and Monte Carlo methods become appropriate. The Multiple Variate Counter (Colin, 1961, 1963, 1964) is concerned primarily with the reduction of raw data from surveys, etc, to its statistical parameters. Montecode (Kelly and Buxton, 1962) provides for use of Monte Carlo methods for computations involving stochastic variables. Mention should also be made of Autostat (Douglas, 1960) and its extended form Opal (Pilling, 1963); the latter is a simulation language with provision for stochastic variables.

Simulation languages (Freeman, 1964) include GPSS, Simscript and CSL (see also Buxton, 1962), and the Elliott Simulation Package (Williams, 1964). The first three of these are IBM developments; GPSS caters for those who prefer to think in terms of block diagrams, Simscript for those requiring Fortran in the computational aspects, while CSL (a British development) suits problems with elaborate logical situations. The Elliott Simulation Package takes the form of extra facilities associated with the Elliott Algol compiler.

It is no disparagement on a similation language to describe it as a conversion kit to turn some existing language into something bigger and better. (If anything, it is an implied criticism of the standard language.) The simulation which is carried out in these languages is that of real time processes such as queueing, workshop scheduling, chemical processes or military exercises. For a neat handling of such problems a master programme which handles the time is required, and entries to this programme must be by standard features of the language. Besides holding the variable which represents the time and making it available to other routines on a read-only basis, this programme must maintain a diary into which other routines can write; in general, its mode of operation will be to advance the time to the next diary-entry, update variables which change continuously, and call the routine represented by the diary entry, unless the updating process reveals an earlier, unforeseen event, in which case it advances the time only to the latter. (E.g. routine *heater on* could enter *water boiling* in the diary for 5 minutes later, or it could set a non-zero rate of change of *water-temperature*, in which case integration of the latter must never be allowed to carry it above 100°C.) Williams (loc. cit.) gives a complete programme for a waiting room, several doctor, queueing problem, which illustrates the type of situation which is met in these languages.

Control languages are closely related to simulation languages. On-line control languages have been developed for military purposes. Machine tool control languages are usually off-line; that is, a description of the work required is translated into the machine language of the tool, on tape, and the tape fed to the tool. The primary language contains provision for various descriptions — e.g. a circle in terms of three points or in terms of centre and radius. An early language in

140

this class, Apt, was developed by R.A.E. Farnborough; information on the later ones is usually to be obtained from the manufacturers of the associated tool control equipment.

15.2 New facilities

The 'main stream' languages do not differ very much in what they enable one to do, but rather in matching the means of saying what is to be done, to the set of likely problems and to the character sets and other features of the equipments. Every now and then one comes across something in one language which cannot be said in another without going into machine code. Again, there are peculiar idioms which enable one to ask for things which are only special cases of a general facility which might be useful. These are pointers to areas in which programming languages as a whole might benefit by further extensions. It is the purpose of this section to list some of these. They are items which maintenance committees talk about, rather than items which appear in current languages.

15.2.1 Environmental inquiries

Naur (1964) has suggested, in an attempt to make Algol more machine independent but with an eye on wider application, provision of certain standard functions whose values are characteristic of the equipment being used. In this way an Algol programme could inquire of the precision of a real variable and go into double length working only if it was necessary on the particular machine being used; a Cobol programme could inquire how many tapes are available, instead of having the number specified in the environment division, and so on.

15.2.2 Variable inquiries

A similar suggestion would provide for retrieval of information other than its value concerning a variable — e.g. its precision, its type, and so on. In the case of arrays, dimensionality and size can be asked for. Odd items in this list can already be demanded in certain languages, but no attempt at systematic study of the requirements seems to have been undertaken. Note that an inquiry as to the type of a variable amounts to an assignment to a variable of type **type** (unless type is coded by mapping on to the integers, which is undesirable for reasons appearing in the next section) and that this is a new type of variable, although foreshadowed by the special case involved in CPL's function *Formarray*.

15.2.3 Generalized type manipulation

Practically all languages say what they have to say in terms of a limited number of infixed operators supplemented by the functional notation of function-name followed by arguments in brackets. A type may be defined loosely as the set of all objects which react in the

141

same manner when under control of the infixed operators. This definition is adequate to indicate what is required to permit the definition by the programmer of types additional to those defined by the semantics of the language itself. Provision of this facility is another feature which is not to be found in any existing language, but is being discussed in some quarters. Its general availability would embrace the special case of matrix algebra which has been a bone of contention for some time.

15.2.4 Open-ended languages

By open-endedness we mean that property, shown by natural languages, by which they are able to describe possible changes in their own structure and then adopt them, at least temporarily, in order the better to deal with situations not envisaged when the language was first developed. In as fully developed form as we find this in natural languages, it is probably too powerful a tool for us to handle properly as yet, but there are significant signs of a gradual feeling of our way towards this sort of facility.

The facility in PL/I by which statements preceded by '%' are to be obeyed at compile time, while intended for the purpose of providing a macro-facility, is actually wider in its scope and is a step in this direction. When this facility is used the 'source text' must begin with a '%DECLARE. . .' statement in which all identifiers to be used at compile time are declared (integer or character string), and possibly initialized; these are known as macro-variables. The remainder of the source-text is then converted into 'programme text' by (1) copying plain text, (2) substituting values for macro-variables, and (3) obeying macro-instructions. Substitution can be recursive and obedience can generate loops by means of macro-labels, macro-conditionals and macro-'go-to's. Parameter notation is not used at the macro level; instead, the concatenation operator is used with string constants and variables. (This would involve our first example of the use of Macrogenerator being written

    % DECLARE VERSE, ANIMAL, SOUND (CHARACTER VARYING);
    % VERSE = 'Old Macdonald . . . had some' || ANIMAL || . . . ;
    % ANIMAL = 'chicks';
    % SOUND = 'cheep';
    VERSE;

and so on.) During this process the source text remains unaltered. When its end is reached, macro-activity ceases and the programme-text, which contains no macro-material, is then compiled. (So the true equivalent of Macrogenerator would be a programme which compiled a single print statement, and not as above.)

Radin and Rogoway make it clear that the use of the same language for macro-operation as is used for the programme itself is a

142

deliberate attempt at a first step towards an open-ended language, and they give an example in which string manipulation is used in an advanced way, namely, if a function $f(p,q)$ involves p being an expression and q its derivative, the work of derivation can be performed by the macro-facility. At the same time, the first-step character of this facility is clear from such features as the lack of block structure at the macro-level (all macro-variables must be declared in the first statement of all), the fact that macro-parameters are handled by the **perform** technique of Section 11.1 and so on.

A first step in a different direction is provided by XPOP (Halpern 1964, 1966). XPOP is not so much a language as a linguistic facility which could be attached to any language; it has been developed with Fap, the symbolic assembly code for a number of IBM machines, which is not unlike the Assembly language in Section 9.2, except that there is no accumulator field because the machines have only one accumulator. The facilities provided by XPOP fall into three groups:

1. Extensions of Fap
2. Systems facilities — for use within the compiling machine during the compilation process
3. Notation re-defining facilities

As regards (1), all the extra facilities of XPOP are made available, by means of extra pseudo-operation codes, within the Fap grammar. A macro is 'declared' by writing its 'body', preceded by a pseudo-instruction with the name of the macro as label, MACRO as its operation, and a list of bound variables as its operand, and succeeded by the pseudo-instruction which has END as its operation. XECUTE and COMPYL similarly bracket instructions to be obeyed during compilation. However, the purpose of this facility is for making corrections when debugging, etc, and falls in group (2) above, which really lies outside our purview; it is not to be confused with the more genuinely linguistic purpose of the superficially similar facility in PL/I. The fundamental difference is that PL/I's facility acts within the source programme, whereas XPOP's acts on the compiled programme.

Our interest is in the third group. XPOP was designed with certain needs in mind, which included its use on-line by personnel unfamiliar with programming languages, and accordingly it contains provisions whereby the user can define his own preferred way of saying something. The 'canonical form' of a macro call is, after an optional label, the name of the macro (what was the label of the pseudo-operation MACRO in the definition) followed by its parameters separated by commas and terminated by a blank. The one unchangeable, anchor, feature of this is that the first word is the macro name. This ties the free, users', grammar down to the rule that every statement must begin with its imperative verb — probably the least restrictive rule

143

which it is possible to impose from the point of view of user and compiler alike. For the rest, pseudo-operations exist by which (1) other character combinations can replace or supplement the comma and blank as separators and terminators, and (2) words can be defined to be noisewords — words to be ignored in looking for parameters. Furthermore, these words need not be altogether ignored — they can be defined (a) to represent an omitted parameter, or (b) to cue in parameters which may be out of order (e.g. if ADD adds the first parameter to the second, then if in ADD A TO B, TO is a cue to B, then ADD TO B, A will not be misunderstood on account of the inverted order). The omitted parameter feature, incidentally, is a curious one useful if correctly handled; if it existed in Algol, then the following would illustrate its use

$$\textbf{procedure } increment(x, y, 01); \textbf{ begin}$$
$$x := x+1; \quad y := y+01 \textbf{ end};$$

A call $increment(a,b)$ would increment both a and b by unity, but a call $increment(a,b,c)$ would increment a by 1 and b by c. In a situation like

   begin real x, y, z;
      procedure proc(x,y,z) . . .
      :
      proc(a,,c); . . .

the absence of the second parameter in the call would cause any y in the procedure body to have the meaning which it would have if it were not a formal parameter, viz., here the real variable declared in the first line.

XPOP's claim on its own behalf is that it allows any programmer to develop the programming language most congenial to himself. To be of universal application it would seem to need a 'skeletal language' consisting of a set of macros which would be rewritten in terms of the assembly language of any new machine. The correct selection and definition of these primitive macros is obviously another method of approach to the subject of formal semantics.

15.3 Subsets of English

From time to time the suggestion is made that we might make use of a subset of English for programming. In fact, this was one of the ideas behind Cobol. Looked at in this light, Cobol went completely off the rails. When we say that Basic Fortran is a subset of full Fortran, the idea in this statement is that anything done in Basic Fortran will be judged good full Fortran by any test made up for this purpose. No knowledge of the rules of Basic Fortran is necessary to make this test. But if we give a programme in Cobol to a judge of good English (and there is no need for such a judge to have any knowledge of Cobol), it is probable that he will say that, though it makes use of

144

English words, it is not in English, and it is certain that he will say that it is not *good* English. So Cobol is not a subset of English.

An example of a subset of English is Basic English (cf. Richards, 1943). The discovery of the existence of this useable subset was made in the 1920's by C. K. Ogden. Its vocabulary (word-list) is made up of

100 operations (verbs, prepositions and so on)
600 names (of things and abstract ideas)
150 qualities (adjectives)
 ? special names (proper nouns, technical terms and so on).

If the special names in any one work are kept under 150, the complete vocabulary for that work is kept under 1,000 words. As to the test, if you are a judge of good English and the writing in this section has your approval, then we have taken the test and come through with flying colours.

To see if something is in Basic English, the quickest way is to take a look at its verbs. Among the 100 operations are

be	come	do	get	give	go	have	keep	let
make	may	put	say	see	seem	send	take	will

and these eighteen are the only verbs in Basic English, though the number may seem greater because the forms ⟨noun⟩ing and ⟨noun⟩ed may be used anywhere where an adjective might go whenever the effect of doing so is good full English. It is less simple to be quite certain that one has not gone outside the range of the other operation-words, and less important over the names because of the power to take in special names. In this section we have gone outside only in

programming: giving a machine the details of what it is to do
subset: a group of things which is a part of a greater group. In making a comparison between two languages the 'things' are statements, not words (as is clear both from the Chomsky way of looking at a language and from the way a good judge does his work).
noun, verb, adjective: words which in full English have a sense of naming, doing or quality-giving.

and one or two (as *vocabulary*) whose sense is given at the first place at which they are used.

As Basic English is a language for all purposes, it is more than is needed for programming, even with the 1,000 word vocabulary limit, and its grammar (its rules for putting together statements) is almost as complex as that of full English. The chief profit to the learner is in the field of accidence, not syntax. (From now on we shall make use of any special names whose sense has been given earlier in this book.) It is not free from ambiguities (for example 'He took a picture from the window'). It is important, not as a possible programming language in itself, but (1) as a step in the right direction from the natural language

145

side, and (2) because its small vocabulary (a) makes it more manageable in machine studies of natural languages, and (b) is a help in getting the different questions which have to be answered separate from each other. As an example of (2a), McConologue and Simmons (1965) give an account of a 'Pattern-learning Parser' which was quicker in learning when given material in Basic English (from Richards and Gibson (1960)) than when given material in normal English. (But the chief purpose of their work is in the field of machine translation, not in that of programming languages, because it was hoped that processes which give success quickly in a simple language will give success in the long run with other languages.)

It is worth the space of a single paragraph (in normal English) to conclude with the observation that while nothing can dim the technical achievement which Basic English represents, politically it met with catastrophe. There was a moment during the second world war when Churchill was interested in it as a world language, but copyright laws were invoked to preserve its purity, prevent the rise of dialects, and so on, and this killed it (politically) far more effectively than either the arguments or the ridicule of its opponents could do. There is a moral here somewhere for all who seek proprietary rights in programming languages.

15.3.1 Pronouns

Any attempt to construct a language which reads smoothly like a subset of a natural language very soon meets the fact that it cannot be done without pronouns. It would appear that the whole question of pronouns is a major bridge to be crossed in linking programming languages (as they now are) and natural languages. Their limited introduction into programming languages would have certain advantages. The nearest approach so far implemented is probably a feature of Nebula known as 'q' or 'quantity-in-hand'. This is a working variable whose value can be deduced from a knowledge of what happened in the previous statement. After an assignment, it is the value handed over. Therefore, if '$z := x; y := x+1$' is replaced by '$z := x; y := q+1$', the time of a second store access for x is saved. The second statement reads 'make z equal to x and y equal to *this* plus one'. Another move in this direction is the proposal by Hill (1965) to introduce **self** into Algol. This may only be used on the r.h.s. of assignment statements with a single l.h.s., and it refers to the l.h.s. Replacement of $x := x+1$ by $x :=$ **self**$+1$ has few advantages, but in

$$A[p - q, p+q] := \textbf{self} + 1$$

it avoids both rewriting and recomputing of a complicated expression. Should one take this further — e.g. $A[p - q, p+q] := B[\textbf{ibid}]+1$?

A comparison between verbal instructions such as 'Take x, increase *it* **by** *1* and store *it* in y', or 'Evaluate. . . ; multiply *this* by. . . ' , and

146

any machine code equivalents will show a high correlation between use of pronouns in the natural language and retention of a result in an accumulator (if possible) at machine code level. The chief difficulty in applying the principle of pronouns is the extent to which semantic considerations rather than syntactic ones are used in determining the antecedent of a pronoun. As an extreme example, consider the two sentences

(a) The committee considered that the meat was safe because it contained an adequate amount of preservative.
(b) The committee considered that the meat was safe because it found an adequate amount of preservative.

The antecedent of 'it' can only be determined by the verb which *follows* the 'it', and then only by knowledge of the fact that meat cannot find things, and committees do not (we hope) contain preservative. Yet both sentences on their own are perfectly clear.

15.4 Ross's Algorithmic theory of language

In view of the many questions referred to or implied by the foregoing discussions, we conclude with an account of an alternative to pure CBN theory which promises to come to grips with the semantic-syntactical interactions with which formal grammar alone cannot deal. In his *Algorithmic Theory of Language*, Ross (1962, 1964) aims at a decision algorithm for natural languages. He divides the terminal vocabulary into two representative groups which he calls *symbols* and *words*, but which we shall call *objects* and *operators* respectively, since (a) Ross's use produces an unfortunate inversion of the natural association of these terms when applied to programming languages, and (b) the two classes are very close to those distinguished by Ogden in Basic English. Thus a *symbol*, or *object*, is an item in the terminal vocabulary which stands for something in the external world, such as *x*, or *cost*, while a *word*, or *operator*, is an item whose significance is more internal to the language and to the sentence syntax, such as '$+$', ';', **let** or **be**. In Chomsky terms he then assumes

$$\langle \text{construct} \rangle ::= \langle \text{operand} \rangle \langle \text{operator} \rangle \langle \text{operand} \rangle$$
$$\langle \text{operand} \rangle ::= \langle \text{object} \rangle | \langle \text{construct} \rangle | \langle \text{nil} \rangle$$

a highly ambiguous grammar from which the ambiguities are removed by methods which, superficially at least, are foreign to the Chomsky theory. As this grammar stands, it imposes the restriction that two objects cannot occur in succession in a terminal string. Natural languages do not altogether accept this restriction (even when punctuation is included), but formal compliance can usually be achieved by assuming the existence of implicit operators in certain standard situations. The converse case, of two operators in succession, is covered by the nil operand. It is worth noting that in English:

147

1. 'the' almost always has a nil left-hand operand, the exceptions being structures like 'Jack the Ripper'.
2. The commonest need for an implicit operator occurs between an adjective and its noun, or between adjectives when there is no comma.
3. Auxiliary verbs are operators, and so are some main verbs (including all the Basic eighteen); participles are objects when used adjectivally. Between these there is an area where there is room for debate.

The resolution of ambiguity is based on a dictionary of properties. This includes, for any object, a 'type', and for any operator (1) a type for the construct whose centre it is, and (2) a statement about the types it 'likes' to have on either side. When there are no alternatives, an operator can be used to denote the type it produces — e.g. we can use '×' to denote type *product* unless we wish to make finer distinctions such as real product and integer product. As an example, consider the rudimentary dictionary

		on its left	on its right
+	likes	$+, \times,),$ L, N	$\times,),$ L
×	likes	$), $ L	$\times,),$ L
:=	likes	$)^*,$ L	$:=, +, \times,),$ L
)	likes	(only	N only
(	likes	L, N	$+, \times,),$ L

where L denotes a letter, and N denotes *nil*. This dictionary is sufficient to determine, for example, that

$$y := a \times b + c$$

must be interpreted in the sense $(y) := ((a \times b) + c)$, or, as Ross would express it, by the first of the following diagrams:

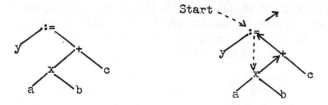

The interpretation $y := (a \times (b+c))$ is impossible because × does not like + on its right, and interpretations like $(y := a) \times (b+c)$ are impossible because × does not like := on its left. Note also that

'nil' on the left of '+' allows for unary '+',

+ on its own left only, but × on its own right only, will guarantee that + associates to the left and × to the right.

If round and square brackets are distinguished as in Algol, then both occur everywhere as shown except (1) each closer likes only its *own* opener on its left, (2) the asterisked bracket is only square (subscripted variables but not functions on the l.h.s. of assignments — unless *car*, *cdr* type functions have round brackets), and (3) a square opener does not like 'nil' on its left.

:= on the right of itself allows for multiple assignments, and maintains the rule that an assignee is a left-hand object.

This illustration is confined to simple numerical assignments; more generally, 'likes' may be dynamic — thus ':=' likes to have on its right the same type of quantity as is already determined to be on its left-hand side, the type of a '+' can be determined to be real or integer by inspection of the types of its operands, and types can be set by declarations.

It is fairly obvious that in simpler cases the 'likes' in the dictionary are equivalent to a set of productions. However, the ':= rule is equivalent to a *set* of productions which the CBN notation can only define by enumeration, thus lacking some flexibility and running the risk (as happened in Algol) that legitimate expressions may become illegal by reason of their accidental omission in the enumeration. The other dynamic type assignments also take in their stride the Λ-productions of Section 7.4.

Ross's full analytical procedure produces the additional information in the second of the above diagrams. Here, the arrows convey the order in which 'evaluation' must proceed, a dotted arrow implying a 'tactical excursion'. Thus, in our illustration, one starts by realizing that an assignment is called for. It takes place 'to' y, which is simple, but to find 'what' is to be assigned to y, one must first do a multiplication (of a by b), then an addition (of the result to c), and then we return to ':=', indicating that the assignment can now be completed and we can proceed to whatever comes next. Note that in Ross's concept, assignment is evaluation, just as much as is addition or multiplication. Evaluation seems an odd word to apply to most sentences in natural languages; compare, however, the process of obtaining the meaning of

The hand that rocked the cradle has kicked the bucket!

Here it is only the final stage of emotional response to which the word 'evaluation' seems at all inappropriate.

15.4.1 The parsing algorithm

The algorithm is a one-pass process, a feature very much in its favour, since passages in natural languages are certainly assimilated in one pass in most cases, and the exceptional cases are deprecated — one should not have to read a passage twice to understand it unless the sense itself is difficult to assimilate. A simple algorithm yields the first, or parsing, diagram and is expanded by grafting further stages on to it to yield the second, or precedence, diagram. The grafting process seems able to accept complication after complication without

149

getting into a position in which it requires a second pass. The degrees of complication admitted may be held to define nesting classes of languages.

A preprocessor (all within the one pass) converts the true input into a series of pointers into the dictionary, and supplements those which point to operators with four tag-pointers, all initially pointing to 'nil' and destined ultimately to hold pointers from the tagged operator to

(a) The word below it and to the left (the left-parsing pointer)
(b) the word below it and to the right (the right-parsing pointer)
(c) The word at the far end of a full arrow (the major precedence pointer) and
(d) The word at the far end of a dotted arrow (the minor precedence pointer).

The parsing algorithm, which sets the first two pointers, may be described as follows. Suppose the input string is ...(V)WXY..., V having just been read. The algorithm is concerned with the top of a stack and with two other variables, M and N, the latter of which will contain V. Representing these as

$$\begin{array}{cc} \text{Stack} & \text{M \quad N} \\ \text{P Q R S T} & \text{U \quad V} \end{array}$$

with T the top of the stack, then there occurs what is called 'a fight between T and V over U', with one of two possible results:

Result R: P Q R S   T   V   U becomes the right operand of T; unload T.

Result L: P Q R S T V   nil   W   U becomes the left operand of V; stack V.

Following result L, if W is an object but not otherwise, a further input occurs leading to

P Q R S T V   W   X

(unless X is also an object, in which case it must be held back and an implicit operator inserted if possible, otherwise the input must be declared ungrammatical). The decision between these two results is taken on the basis of two tests:

TEST I: If T likes U on its right but
           U does not like V on its left . . . . . Result R?
           If V likes U on its left but
           T does not like V on its right . . . . Result L?
           If one of these, accept it; if neither then fail (input is ungrammatical), but if both, then go to Test II.

In Test II; made when both 'likes' in Test I are 'on', the choice is made in such a way as will forestall trouble later, namely,

TEST II: If V does not like T on its left . . . . . Result L
           Else if T does not like V on its
           right, then . . . . Result R

If neither of these criteria is sufficient to force a conclusion, then the situation remains officially ambiguous at this level. Ultimately the stack is cleared, and enough pointers will then have been set to determine the structure. A few remain holding 'nil'; thus in the analysis of $x := (a+b) \times c$, the left-hand pointer of '(' points to 'nil'– it would point to f in the analysis of $x := f(a+b) \times c$.

15.4.2 The precedence algorithm

The simplest precedence algorithm needs no further semantic information. It uses a private pointer which points initially to the first operator pointer in the input string. The setting of a precedence pointer is always made (a) *from* (i.e. in a tag of) the operator thus pointed to, (b) to point *to* an operator involved in a fight, (c) the private pointer then being altered to point to the latter. If the fight is 'over' an object, then no precedence pointer is set unless (a) the result of the fight is to set a right-hand parsing pointer, and (b) the left-hand pointer of the winner is also an object; in this case the minor precedence pointer is set to point to the winner. If the fight was over an operator, a major precedence pointer is always set to point to the winner (this pointer is usually the reverse of the parsing pointer set at the same time). The following sequence shows how this works out in the case of the sentence $y := a \times b + c$:

Stack	M	N	Result of I	II	Parsing ptr set	Precedence ptr set
nil	y	:=	L		y ← :=	
:–	a	×		L	a ← ×	
:=	b	+		R	× → b	:= – → ×
:=	×	+		L	× ← +	× → +
:= +	c	End	R		+ → c	
:=	+	End	R		:= → +	+ → :–

and the final state in the machine can best be represented by

Contents of loc:	0	1	2	3	4	5	6	7
point to:	Start	y	:=	a	×	b	+	c
Tag 'a' holds	nil		1		3		4	
'b'	nil		6		5		7	
'c'	nil		End		6		2	
'd'	2		4		nil		nil	

It has been necessary to describe the above in fair detail in order to make any sense whatever of Ross's extensions to wider classes of languages. His first step is the introduction of 'minor modifiers', which are words that can influence the meaning of operators occurring later in the sentence. Suppose one could write

$$; matrix \ y := a \times b + c;$$

then it is important *not* to arrange for the precedence to go straight to

151

the heart of the matter (which is :=) without taking note of *matrix* first, since this affects the meaning of both := and the arithmetic signs. In this context, *matrix* will be an operator with a *nil* l.h.s., and the minor precedence pointer which the former rules would set from the first *;* to the :=, must be broken in such a way as to call at *matrix* 'en route'.

The second step is the much bigger one of introducing likes and dislikes into the precedence-setting part of the algorithm. This involves another stack on which to keep completed fragments of the precedence chain which so far cannot be linked into anything bigger. For an intuitive perception of what this means, consider the following, in the idiom suggested at the end of Section 14.7:

begin . . . **end**, termbyterm;

It means that the syntax of any part of the contents of the compound statement can be sorted out as we scan it, and yet the result kept in suspense as regards its semantics until it is known whether any option has been stated. It permits the precedence chain to look ahead and treat *termbyterm* as if it preceded the **begin**, like *matrix* in the previous paragraph. It provides a simple mechanism for single scan comprehension of sentences full of forward references such as

Although it was raining cats and dogs, and, falling being now apparently part of its nature, the barometer held out no prospect of relief, once he had put on his greatcoat and oilskins, the captain felt warm and dry inside and prepared to brave the elements indefinitely

— a style which may be deplored, but is used.

It will be seen that all of this leaves the original syntactic structure (as determined by the parsing algorithm) untouched, but consists of modifications with profound effects on the precedence chain. It would seem, therefore, that Ross is developing a 'structural semantics' midway between syntax and 'operational semantics'; a formalized 'semantic grammar' for getting out of a sentence the order in which it implies you do things independently of defining exactly what it is you do. This is not a process which can be carried to completion, however, if a language is self-defining even to the degree implied by Algol declarations.

15.4.3 Further comments

The elementary part of Ross's treatment, at least, makes no contribution whatever to one problem — that of determining when two different sentences have identical results (or meaning). For it is possible from his parse to reconstruct the original sentence by the following algorithm:

Start at the top of the diagram.

A: Move as many steps down and to the left as possible.

B: Print what you find.
If there is a move of one step down and to the right, make it and go to A, otherwise
C: If there is a move of one step up and to the right, make it and go to B, otherwise
Move up and to the left as far as possible and go to C. If this is impossible, the process is complete.

Thus it is hopeless to expect the fact that two alternative word orders convey identical meaning (if they do) to declare itself in the two orders leading to the same diagram. But a number of avenues remain. (1) There may be— indeed there are — operators which are known to be symmetrical. (2) The sequence in the precedence chain may reveal equivalences. (3) In some situations a modifier can imply some implicit syntax change — a well-known case of this being those words which, when they start a sentence, cause inversion later on.

The concept of a fight is confirmed by some unpublished work of the author. Consider the structure 'The A of the B', where the alternatives for B include the structure itself. A recursive structure of this sort can be expanded without limit, in practice as well as theory. We have no difficulty in understanding

The election of the chairman of the committee of the society of the friends of the cathedral

nor is there any doubt that the structure is correctly interpreted by the recursive definition. It is the election of something, and that something is the chairman of something. It is not

The committee-etc's election-of-the-chairman

nor any other alternative structure. But now consider

The effect of the election of the chairman of the committee of the society of the friends of the cathedral was unfortunate.

All our previous comments hold. But if *any* one of the *of*s is replaced by *on*, its effect is to take one right back to the word *effect* for a new link. My interpretation of this is that *effect* 'expects' both *of* and *on*. Having got its *of*, its expectation in that direction is satisfied, but the expectation of *on* remains until one of three things happens. (a) All expectations are cancelled by the end of the sentence. (b) If another word that expects *on* intervenes, a fight may occur. (c) But otherwise the expectation will exert itself as soon as an *on* appears. The second possibility, of a fight, led to a game. This is to start with a construction which is syntactically ambiguous, and with two cases of it which are unhesitatingly parsed differently, and then to modify the variables in it until the tensions are as nearly equal as possible. The results vary from the mildly amusing to the positively disconcerting. Two examples must suffice.

1. *The A of the B of the C.* In 'The election of the chairman of the committee', we clearly have the election of an officer, not an act of the committee. In 'The knowledge of the law of the magistrates' we are unlikely to adopt the interpretation that the magistrates have a special law of their own, and we therefore adopt the admittedly unusual parse with little difficulty. Roughly equal tensions are mildly amusing in 'The Minister of the Interior of the Prince', and positively disconcerting in 'The lilies of the valley of the shadow of death'.
2. *Effect of* and *effect on.* The parsing naturally takes different courses in 'The effect of the election on the people', and 'The mayor of the town on the river'. To counteract the expectation created by *effect*, one needs a fairly close-bonding *on*, as in 'The effect of The Mill on the Floss', or 'The effect of the prisoner on the rack'. A case where equal tensions are held undecided pending further clues can be seen in the way an identical first phrase is differently analysed in the two sentences

The effect of the paint on the wall is to make the wall waterproof.

The effect of the paint on the wall is to reduce the value of the house.

— and even so, one is left with a probabilistic decision which could be reversed by features in a wider context.

Quantification of these ideas in a way which would enable an algorithm to be written would involve maintaining a table of expectations which have been awakened, and provision to make them decay with time (= distance along the scan). There is also required a much more complex theory of types than suffices for programming languages, since it is the type complexity of words like 'mayor', 'town', 'river' when compared with words like 'age', 'cost', 'time', which provides the spectrum of possible, but varyingly probable, readings of many English sentences. For this reason, the use of a subset of a natural language for programming is not as difficult a problem as some of the above considerations might suggest. All the same, it is quite difficult enough.

BIBLIOGRAPHY

This bibliography includes all the references from within the text of this book, and a few others. Attention is drawn particularly to the IEEE Transactions on Electronic Computers for August 1964 (Vol. EC-13, pp. 343–462), 'The Special Issue on Computer Languages' which contains several extensive bibliographies for further reference.

Backus, J. (1959). 'The syntax and semantics of the proposed international algebraic language of the Zurich ACM-GAMM conference' in *Proc. Int. Conf. Inf. Processing*, UNESCO, June 1959, pp. 125–132. Reprinted in *Ann. Rev. in Automatic Programming*, Vol. 1, pp. 268–291 (Pergamon Press, 1961).

Bar Hillel, Y., Perles, M. and Shamir, E. (1961). 'On formal properties of simple phrase structure grammars.' *Z. Phonetik, Sprachwiss. und Kommunikationsforschung, 14*. pp. 143–172.

Barrett, W. and Mitchell, A. J. (1963). 'An extended autocode for Pegasus.' *Computer J., 6*, p. 237.

Barron, D. W., Buxton, J. N., Hartley, D. F., Nixon, E. and Strachey, C. (1963). 'The main features of CPL.' *Computer J., 6*. pp. 134–143.

Bobrow, D. G. (1963). 'Syntactic analysis of English by computer — a survey.' *Proc. 1963 Fall J.C.C.*, Spartan Books, Vol. 24 pp. 365–387.

Bobrow, D. G. and Raphael, B. (1964). 'A comparison of list processing languages.' *C.A.C.M., 7*, pp. 231–240.

Borko, H. (Editor) (1962). *Computer Application in the Behavioral Sciences.*

Brooker, R. A. (1956). 'The programming strategy used with the Manchester University Mk.I computer.' *Proc. I.E.E.*, Vol. 103B, Supplement, pp. 151–157.

Brooker, R. A., and Morris, D. (1960). 'An assembly program for a phrase structure language.' *Computer J., 3*, pp. 168–179.

Brooker, R. A., and Morris, D. (1962). 'A description of Mercury Autocode in terms of a phrase structure language.' *Ann. Rev. in Automatic Programming, 2*, pp. 29–65 (Pergamon Press).

Brooker, R. A., and Morris, D. (1963). 'A general translation program for phrase structure languages.' *J.A.C.M. 9*, pp. 1–10.

Brooker, R. A., McCallum, I. R., Morris, D., and Rohl, J. S., (1963).

'The Compiler compiler.' *Ann. Rev. in Automatic Programming*, *3*, pp. 229–275 (Pergamon Press). See also an article in *J.A.C.M.*, *9*, pp. 1–10 (1962).

British Standards Institution. 'Glossary of terms used in Data processing.'

Burkhardt, W. H. (1965). 'Metalanguage and syntax specification.' *C.A.C.M.*, *8*, pp. 304–305. See also a letter in *ibid* p. 261.

Buxton, J. N., and Laski, J. C. (1962). 'Control and simulation language.' *Computer J.*, *5*, pp. 194–199.

Caracciolo di Forino, A. (1963). *C.A.C.M.*, *6*, pp. 456–460.

Chomsky, N. (1956). 'Three models for the description of language.' *I. R. E. Trans. Inf. Theory*, *2*, pp. 113–124.

— (1957). *Syntactic Structures*. Mouton, The Hague.

— (1959). 'On certain formal properties of grammars', *Inf. and Control*, *2*, pp. 137–167. Also 'A note on phrase-structure grammars', *ibid*, pp. 393–395.

— (1962). 'Formal properties of grammars' in *Handbook of Mathematical psychology* (ed. R. R. Bush, E. H. Gelernter and R. D. Luce) Vol. 2, Ch. 12.; Wiley, New York.

Chomsky, N., and Schützenberger, M. P. (1963). 'The algebraic theory of context-free languages' in *Computer programming and formal systems* (ed. Braffort and Hirschberg), North-Holland Pub. Co., Amsterdam; pp. 118–161.

Church, A. (1941). *The Calculi of Lambda Conversion*. Princeton University Press.

Clarke, B., and Felton, G. F. (1959). 'The Pegasus Autocode.' *Computer J.*, *1*, p. 192.

Cohen, K., and Wegstein, J. H. (1965). 'Axle: an axiomatic language for string transformation.' *C.A.C.M.* *8*, pp. 657–661.

Colin, A. J. T. (1961). 'MVC Mark 3: A general survey analysis program for Mercury.' University of London Computer Unit Internal Report.

— (1963). 'The MVC manual.' University of London Computer Unit Internal Report.

— (1964). 'The multiple variate counter.' *Computer J.*, *6*, pp. 339–347.

Conway, R. W., Delfausse, J. J., Maxwell, W. L., and Walker, W. E. (1965). 'CLP — the Cornell List Processor.' *C.A.C.M.* *8*, pp. 215–216. (Includes a brief account of CORC, in which CLP is embedded.)

Cooper, D. C. and Whitfield, H. (1962). 'ALP, An autocode list-processing language.' *Computer J.*, *5*, pp. 28–31.

Corbato, F. J. (1963). *The Compatible Time sharing System and Programmers' Guide*. M.I.T. Press.

Curry, H. B., and Feys, R. (1958). *Combinatory Logic*, Vol. 1 North-Holland Pub. Co., Amsterdam.

Davis, M. (1958). *Computability and Unsolvability*. McGraw-Hill.

156

Dickens, C. (1837). *The Posthumous Papers of the Pickwick Club*, Nelson Edition, p. 147.

Dijkstra, E. W. (1962). 'An Algol translator for the X1' in *Automatic Programming Bulletin*, No. 13, reprinted in *Ann. Rev. in Automatic Programming*, *3*, pp. 329–356 (1963).

Dijkstra, E. W. (1963). 'On the design of machine independent programming languages.' *Ann. Rev. in Automatic Programming 3*, pp. 27–42.

Douglas, A. S., and Mitchell, A. J. (1960). 'Autostat: A language for statistical programming.' *Computer J. 3*, p. 61.

Duncan, F. G. (1963). 'Input and Output for Algol 60 on KDF9.' *Computer J. 5*, p. 341.

Edelstein, L. A. (1963). 'Picture logic for Bacchus, a fourth generation computer.' *Computer J. 6*, p. 144. (No language here, but a new field that may call for one.)

Eickel, J., Paul, M., Bauer, F., and Samelson, K. (1963). 'A syntax controlled generator of formal language processors.' *C.A.C.M.*, *6*, pp. 451–455.

Elgot, C. C., and Robinson, A. (1964). 'Random access stored-program machines, an approach to Programming languages.' *J.A.C.M. 11*, pp. 365–400.

Farber, D. J., Griswold, R. E., and Polonsky, I. P. (1964). 'Snobol: A string manipulation language.' *J.A.C.M. 11*, pp. 21–30.

Feldman, J. (1964). 'A formal semantics for computer oriented languages.' Doctoral Dissertation, Carnegie Inst. of Tech.

Floyd, R. W. (1961). 'A descriptive language for symbol manipulation.' *J.A.C.M. 8*, pp. 579–584.

— (1962). 'On the non-existence of a phrase structure grammar for Algol 60.' *C.A.C.M. 5*, p. 483.

— (1963). 'Syntactic analysis and operator precedence.' *J.A.C.M. 10*, pp. 316–333.

— (1964). 'Bounded context syntactic analysis.' *C.A.C.M. 7*, pp. 62–65.

Freeman, D. E. (1964). 'Programming languages ease digital simulation.' *Control Engineering*, Nov. 1964, pp. 103–106.

Fries, C. C. (1952). *The Structure of English*. Longmans Green.

Garwick, J. (1964). 'Gargoyle, a language for compiler writing.' *C.A.C.M.*, Jan. 1964.

Gelernter, H., Hansen, J. R., and Gerberich, C. C. (1960). 'A Fortran-compiled list-processing language.' *J.A.C.M.*, 7 (1961), pp. 87–101.

Gilmore, P. C. (1963). 'An abstract computer with a Lisp-like machine language without a label operator.' pp. 71–86 of *Computer Programming and Formal Systems* (ed. Braffort, P., and Hirschberg, D.) North-Holland Pub. Co., Amsterdam.

Ginsberg, S., and Rice, H. C. (1962). 'Two families of languages related to Algol.' *J.A.C.M.*, *9*, pp. 350–371.

157

Ginsberg, S., and Rose, G. F. (1963). 'Some recursively unsolvable problems in Algol-like languages.' *J.A.C.M. 10*, pp. 29–47. Also 'Operations which preserve definability in languages', *ibid*, pp. 175–195.

Goodman, R. (Editor) (1963). 'Automatic Programming Bulletin, No. 17.' Brighton Technical College.

Gorn, S. (1963). 'The detection of generative ambiguities in context-free languages.' *J.A.C.M., 10*, pp. 196–208.

Greibach, S., (1964). 'Formal Parsing Systems.' *C.A.C.M. 7*, pp. 499–504.

— (1965). 'A new normal form theorem for C.F.P.S. grammars.' *J.A.C.M., 12*, pp. 42–52.

Griffiths, T. V., and Petrick, S. R. (1965). 'On the relative efficiencies of context-free grammar recognisers.' *C.A.C.M. 8*, pp. 289–300.

Halpern, M. I. (1964). 'XPOP: a Meta-language without metaphysics.' *Proc. Fall Joint Computer Conf. 1964*, pp. 57–68.

— (1966): forthcoming paper in *Ann. Rev. in Automatic Programming* Vol. 5.

Heising, W. P. (1965). Report of American Standards Association, ASA Committee X3, published in *C.A.C.M. 7*, p. 10, ibid pp. 591–625, and *C.A.C.M. 8*, pp. 287–8.

Higman, B. (1963) 'Towards an Algol translator.' *Ann. Rev. in Automatic Programming, 3*, pp. 121–162. Pergamon Press.

Hill, I. D. (1965). *Algol Bulletin* No. 21, pp. 70–74.

Hornby, A. S. (1954). *A Guide to Patterns and Usage in English.* Oxford University Press.

Huskey, H. D. (1961). 'Compiling Techniques for Algebraic Expressions.' *Computer J. 4*, p. 10. See also *C.A.C.M. 3*, pp. 463–468 (1960) and *6*, pp. 649–658 (1963).

I.F.I.P. 'Report on input/output procedures for Algol.' Reprinted in *C.A.C.M. 7*, pp. 628/630.

Iliffe, J. K. (1961). 'The use of the Genie system in numerical calculations.' *Ann. Rev. in Automatic Programming, 2*, pp. 1–28.

Iliffe, J. K., and Jodeit, J. C. (1962). 'A dynamic storage allocation scheme.' *Computer J., 5*, pp. 200–209.

Irons, E. T. (1961). 'A syntax-directed compiler for Algol 60'. *C.A.C.M. 4*, pp. 51–55.

— (1963). 'The structure and use of the syntax directed compiler.' *Ann. Rev. in Automatic Programming, 3*, pp. 207–227.

— (1964). 'Structural connections in formal languages.' *C.A.C.M. 7*, 67–71.

Iverson, K. E. (1962). *A Programming Language.* John Wiley and Sons, N.Y.

— (1964). 'A method of syntax specification.' *C.A.C.M., 7*, pp. 588–589.

Kelley, D. H., and Buxton, J. N. (1962). 'Montecode — an inter-

158

pretive program for Monte Carlo simulation.' *Computer J.*, *5*, pp. 88–93.

Kleene, S. C. (1952). *Introduction to Metamathematics*. Van Nostrand.

Knuth, D. E. (1964a). 'A proposal for i/o conventions in Algol 60.' Report of A.C.M. committee, reproduced in *C.A.C.M. 7*, pp. 273–283.

— (1964b). 'Backus Normal form vs Backus Naur form.' *C.A.C.M. 7*, 735.

Kuno, S., and Oettinger, A. G. (1962). 'Multiple path syntactic analyser.' *Proc. IFIP Congress*, North-Holland, Amsterdam, pp. 306–312.

— (1963). 'Syntactic structure and ambiguity in English.' *Proc. Fall J. Comp. Conf.* pp. 397–418. Spartan Books, Baltimore.

Kuno, S. (1965). 'The predictive analyser and a path elimination technique.' *C.A.C.M. 8*, pp. 453–462.

Landin, P. (1964). 'The mechanical evaluation of expressions'. *Computer J.*, *6*, pp. 308–320.

— (1965). 'A correspondence between Algol 60 and Church's Lambda-notation.' *C.A.C.M. 8*, Part I: pp. 89–101, Part II: pp. 158–165

Leavenworth, B. M. (1964). 'Fortran IV as a syntax language'. *C.A.C.M.*, *7*, pp. 72–79.

McCarthy, J. (1960). 'Recursive functions of symbolic expressions and their calculation by machine, Part I.' *C.A.C.M.*, *3*, pp. 184–195.

— (1962). *LISP.1.5 Programmer's Manual*. Cambridge, M.I.T.

— (1963). 'A basis for a mathematical theory of computation' in *Computer programming and formal systems*, Amsterdam, North-Holland Pub Co. See also 'Towards a mathematical science of computation' in *Proc. IFIP Munich Conf. 1962*, North Holland, 1963.

McConologue, K., and Simmons, R. F. (1965). 'Analysing English syntax with a pattern learning parser.' *C.A.C.M.*, *8*, pp. 687–698.

Metcalfe, H. H. (1963). 'A parametrized compiler based on mechanical linguistics.' *A.C.M. Nat. Conf.* Denver, Ohio. Reprinted in *Ann Rev in Automatic Programming 4* (1964) pp. 125–165.

Miller, G. A. (1965). Presidential address in The Advancement of Science, Vol. XXI, No. 93, p. 425.

Naur, P. (1960). 'Report on the Algorithmic Language ALGOL 60.' *C.A.C.M.*, *3*, p. 299 or *Numerische Mathematik 2*, p. 106. Revised report (1963) in *Computer J.*, *5*, p. 349, *C.A.C.M.*, *6*, pp. 1–17, or *Ann Rev. in Auto Prog.*, *4*, p. 217. For Algol 58 see Backus (1958).

— (1964). Algol Bulletin No. 18, pp. 26–43.

Newell, A. (1961). *Information Processing Language-V Manual*. The Rand Corporation. See also Newell, A., and Tonge, F. M., *C.A.C.M.*, *3*, p. 205.

159

Opler, A. (1965). 'Procedure-oriented language statements to facilitate parallel processing.' *C.A.C.M.*, *8*, p. 306.

Oettinger, A. G. (1960). *Automatic Language Translation*. Harvard University Press, Cambridge, Mass.

Paterson, J. B. (1963). 'The Cobol Sort Verb.' *C.A.C.M.*, *6*, pp. 255–258

Perlis, A., Smith, J. W., and Evans, A. (1959). 'TASS.' Computation Centre, Carnegie Inst. Tech.

Perlis, A. J. (1964). 'A format language.' *C.A.C.M.*, *7*, pp. 89–96.

Pfeiffer (1960). *Fortune*, May 1960, p. 153.

Pilling, D. (1963). 'C-E-I-R OPAL Language.' C.E.I.R. (U.K.) Ltd, Internal report.

Quine, W. V. (1960). *Word and Object*. New York, John Wiley and Technology Press.

Rabinowitz, I. N. (1962). 'Report on the Algorithmic Language FORTRAN II.' *C.A.C.M.*, *5*, pp. 327–337.

Radin, G., and Rogoway, H. P. (1965). 'NPL: Highlights of a New Programming Language.' *C.A.C.M.*, *8*, pp. 9–17.

Randell, B. (1963). Private communication.

Richards, L. A., and Gibson, C. (1960). *English Through Pictures*, Bk. I., Washington Sq. Press Inc., N.Y.

Richards, I. A. (1943). *Basic English and its uses*. London, Kegan Paul.

Rose, G. F. (1964). 'An extension of Algol-like languages.' *C.A.C.M.*, *7*, pp. 52–60.

Rosen, S. (1964). 'A compiler building system developed by Brooker and Morris.' *C.A.C.M.*, *7*, pp. 403–414.

Ross, D. T. (1959) 'The design and use of the APT language for automatic programming of numerically controlled machine tools.' *Proc. Comp. App. Symposium, ITT Res. Inst.*, Chicago, Ill., pp. 80–99.

— (1962). *On the Algorithmic Theory of Language*. ESL-TM-156, Elec. Systems Lab., M.I.T., Cambridge, Mass.

— (1964). 'On context and ambiguity in parsing.' *C.A.C.M.*

Rossiter, A. P. (1939). 'The growth of science' (in *Basic English*). Pelican Books.

Samelson, K., and Bauer, F. L. (1960) 'Sequential formula translation.' *C.A.C.M.*, *3*, pp. 76–83.

Shavell, Z. A. (1965). 'The use of Fortran in subroutines with Cobol main programs.' *C.A.C.M.*, *8*, pp. 221–2.

Shaw, C. J. (1963). 'A specification of Jovial.' *C.A.C.M.*, *6*, pp. 721–736. Also 'Jovial, A programming language for real time command systems'. *Ann. Rev. in Automatic Programming, 3* (1963), pp. 53–119.

Sproull (1964). Cited from Ref. 6 of Datamation, Dec. 1964, p. 48.

Steel, T. (1964). 'Beginnings of a theory of information handling.' *C.A.C.M.*, *7*, pp. 97–103

Strachey, C. (1965). 'A general purpose macrogenerator.' Cambridge University Math. Lab. Report No. 65/1, reprinted in *Computer J.*, *8*, pp. 225–241.

— (1963). See Barron *et al* (1963).

Strachey, C. and Wilkes, M. V. (1961). 'Some proposals for improving the efficiency of Algol 60.' *C.A.C.M.*, *4*, pp. 488–491.

Tajiri, K. (1965). 'The use of Cobol subroutines in Fortran main programs.' *C.A.C.M.*, *8*, 223–4.

Tocher, K. D. (1960). *Handbook of the General Simulation Program*. United Steel Co., Dept. Op. Res. Report No. 77/ORC 3/Tech.

Weizenbaum, J. (1963). Symmetric List Processor, *C.A.C.M.*, *6*, 524–544.

Wilkes, M. V. (1964). 'An experiment with a self-compiling compiler for a simple list-processing language.' Camb. Univ. Math. Lab. Tech. Memo 63/1, reprinted in *Ann. Rev. in Automatic Programming*, *4*, pp. 1–48.

Williams, J. W. J. (1964). 'E.S.P. The Elliott Simulator Package.' *Computer J.*, *6*, pp. 328–331.

Wirth, N. (1963). 'A generalization of Algol.' *C.A.C.M.*, *6*, pp. 547–554.

Woodger, M. (1963). 'The description of a computing process. Some observations on automatic programming and Algol 60.' *Ann. Rev. in Automatic Programming*, *3*, pp. 1–16.

Woodward, P. M., and Jenkins, D. P. (1961). 'Atoms and lists.' *Computer J.*, *4*, pp. 47–53

Yates, F., and Simpson, H. R. (1960). 'A general program for the analysis of surveys.' *Computer J.*, Part I: *3*, p. 136; Part II, *4*, p. 20.

Yngve, V. H. (1961). *Comit Programmer's Reference Manual*, and *Introduction to Comit Programming*. M.I.T.

161

INDEX

Names of languages are in capitals, names of people in italics. Other entries may be to definitions, special uses of terms in specific languages, or to general discussion; it has not been possible to distinguish these.

162

E-object, 16, 25, 115, 125
Equivalence and Common in Fortran, 73, 116
Error — see Monitor
Escape character (in CPL), 109
Euclid, 10, 95
Evaluation, 34, 91, 149
Expressions, 23–4, 26f, 45, 70, 86, 90f, 110, 124

FACT, 75
FAP, 143
Fight, 150, 153
File, 38, 80, 106, 128, 133f, 137
Filled, 16
Floyd, 43, 48, 49
For — see Loop
Format — see Layout
FORTRAN, 9, 16, 44, 52, 70–74, 95, 127, 130
Function, built-in, 15, 93, 123; Function-generating functions, 120, 124; Function-type variables, 124; Functional languages, 15, 16, 33, 97; see also Procedure.

GARGOYLE, 53
Generic Functions, 119
Gilmore, 30, 32f, 50
Ginsberg, 47, 49
Gorn, 46
Go-to, 2, 11, 17, 28, 39, 66, 71, 83, 98, 120ff
Grammar(s), 7, 13, 41–54, 56, 69, 71, 78, 85, 99, 103, 106ff, 145, 147
Graphic characters, 125
Griffiths und Petrick, 53
GPSS, 140

Hard Copy, 36–37
HARTRAN, 9
Higher-level features, 2, 44, 91, 142–144
Huskey, 50

Iliffe, 25
Imperative, 7, 85f
Indirect Addressing — see Addressing
Infixed operators, 23, 43, 142
Initialising, 82, 83, 108, 112, 115
Input/Output, 36f, 93, 125ff
Interpreter, 1, 98
Intrinsic names, 33
IPL-V, 95, 98–101
Irons, 50, 52
I.S.O. character set, 36, 103, 125; and I/O, 129
Iteration, 18ff, 54, 94
Iverson, 43

Jensen device, 90
JOVIAL, 9, 74
Jump — see 'go to'

Knitting, 10

Label (in Lisp), 97; (of a file), 80; (type name), 17, 28–31, 72, 108, 111; Label–100, 40
Lambda notation and calculus, 27, 33, 47, 97
Landin, 34, 54, 124
Layout, 37, 60, 85, 125ff
Language (general), 7, 33, 41ff; (-s 0 to 3), 41–44
LANGUAGE-H, 75
Leavenworth, 52
Library, 78, 82, 83, 106; See also System routines
Line numbers, 38
Link, 18, 88
LISP, 95–97
List processing languages, 16, 95f, 115, 123; List procedure, 130; List directed output, 134; Lists and list-structures, 93, 95ff; Listed copy, 36
Literals, 30, 31ff, 125
Load and go, 1
L-object, 16, 115, 125
Local variable, 26
Loops, 72, 83, 91, 121f, 128
Lukasiewicz, 23

MAC, 38
Machine code, 1, 3, 65f, 105
Macro(s), 55ff, 124, 143
MACROGENERATOR, 55–64, 97, 129
MAD (MADTRAN), 9
Maintenance, 5, 76, 85
McCarthy, 54, 95
Message, 3
Meta-, 4, 42
Miller, 21
Mixed languages, 39
Modularity, 73, 105
Monitor (and error detection), 1, 3, 58, 68, 73
Multipurpose languages, 14
Multi-processing, 12; See also Parallel processing
MVC, 140

Names, 16, 25ff, 85
Naur, 41, 85, 141
NEBULA, 75
Noise words, 37, 79, 144
Numeral, 3, 31, 32, 34, 59, 85

Obey technique, 13
OPAL, 140
Operand, operator, 26, 33, 43, 54, 147ff; See also Infixed and Prefixed operators
Own (in Algol), 54, 92, 115

Parallel processing, 105, 123
Parameters, 26, 55, 83, 93, 100, 106, 144
Parrots, 14
Parsing Algorithm, 46, 53, 149

163

% (in PL/I), 124, 142
Phrase structure grammars, 45
Place significant notation, 4
PL/I, 102–124, 133f, 142
Polish notation, 23, 33
Pop-up, 97
Precedence grammars, 49; p. algorithm, 151
Prefixed operators, 24
Primitives, 50, 54, 129
Process control, 12, 140
Procedures, 72f, 83, 87f, 117–119; pure, pp, 12, 17, 83; p-al languages, 15, 33f, 86; p-directed output, 135
Productions, 41ff, 51
Programme, 1, 33, 76, 87; p. modification, 12
Pronouns, 13, 146
Push-down, 97

Quotes, 31, 34, 56–60, 109

Radix, 65
RAPIDWRITE, 76
Recognisers, 51
Record — See File
Recursion, 18ff, 27, 33, 57, 84, 90, 112, 118, 123
Reducible grammar, 49
Redundancy, 37
Reentrant routines, 118
Reference — see Calling styles
Relative clauses, 13; See also 'where'
Representative vocabulary, 43ff
Reserved words, 84, 93, 103
Result of . . ., 124
Rose, 47
Ross, 34, 54, 147f
Round-off, 65

Samelson and Bauer, 50
Semantics, 3, 8, 37, 50–54, 57–60, 65, 103, 106, 110, 144; s. reinforcement, 9, 37, 46–47, 147, 152
Sequential grammars, 49
Shift characters, 36
Shillings, 96
SIMSCRIPT, 140
Sited and Siteless, 16
SLIP, 95
SMALGOL, 9
SNOBOL, 139

Sort (verb, in Cobol), 84
Specification, 89
Stack, 23
Statement brackets, 3, 103
Storage, 25, 73, 87
Strachey, 22, 55, 90
String, 3, 33, 93, 125
Structure, 82, 95, 109, 116, 123
Style, 43, 89
Subroutine, open, 124; see also Procedure
Successor function, 20, 59
Suffix, 2, 14
Sugar, 22, 54, 106
Switch, 88, 93, 119f, 127
Symbol (attribute in PL/I), 134; (black type), 2, 85; s. addresses and s. assembly code, see Assembly code
Syntax (definition), 9; see Grammar
System, 1, 38, 40; s. routines, 15, 93, 118

Tape, paper, 36
Tensor calculus, 5
Terminal vocabulary, 41
Theorem proving, 10, 95
Time-sharing, 38, 79
Transformational grammars, 47, 58
Translator, 1
Transparent names, 30
Traps (hardware), 39, 83, 123; (booby), 51, 72, 89
Tree — see Structure
Triangular arrays, 116
Type (of a variable), 87, 111, 141, 154; (of a grammar), 45

Value — see Calling styles
Values, 16, 29–35, 81, 96; see also Evaluation
Variables, 25–35. and *passim*
Vectors, 14, 66
Vocabulary, 7, 41; see also Reserved words
Void, 16, 48, 92

Where, 20, 56ff, 112
WISP, 95, 97–8, 99
Write protection, 31

XPOP, 9, 143

Y-operator, 27, 97

164

Randall Library – UNCW   NXWW

QA76 .5 .H49
Higman / A comparative study of programming langua

304900211436X